GREAT HOUSES

From the Pages of the Magazine ANTIQUES

EDITED AND WITH AN INTRODUCTION BY

CONSTANCE M. GREIFF

THE PYNE PRESS
Princeton

First Edition

Library of Congress Catalog Card Number 73-79522
SBN 87861-054-5, paperbound edition
SBN 87861-053-7, hardcover edition

Cover photograph courtesy of
Historic Charleston Foundation

Manufactured in the United States of America

Distributed by Charles Scribner's Sons, New York

Contents

Introduction

Along with short skirts, bathtub gin and cropped hair, American antiques became fashionable in the 1920s. One harbinger of their popular appeal was the first appearance in 1922 of a magazine dedicated to the interest of connoisseurs, dealers, collectors and curators. Its name, simply The Magazine, *Antiques,* implied that its range would encompass more than Americana. However, the preponderance of articles published in the magazine's first half-century has dealt with objects made in America, or at least with those, like Chinese and English ceramics, which were imported in great quantities to this country. During the 1920s the magazine devoted itself almost entirely to the collector of antiques as individual pieces. It largely ignored the growing concomitant interest in the buildings in which these objects had originally been housed.

This omission was rectified in a somewhat tentative manner in the 1930s. In 1930 *Antiques* published its first article on an American building, a short picture study of the Hammond-Harwood House in Annapolis, Maryland. In August of 1930 a second article appeared, "The Houses of the First Settlers in New England." The author was George Francis Dow, a pioneering New England restorationist. The illustrations included the Parson Capen House in Topsfield, Massachusetts, restored by Dow in 1913, and the House of the Seven Gables in Salem, Massachusetts, restored by him the following year. In a short but scholarly text Dow attacked the popular belief that the early settlers of New England had ever dwelt in log houses akin to those used in the late eighteenth and nineteenth centuries along the American frontier, a theme later exhaustively pursued in Harold Shurtleff's aptly titled book, *The Log Cabin Myth,* published in 1938.

The occasional subsequent articles on architecture that appeared in the 1930s were less theoretical. They followed, rather than led, the interest of the times in dealing with architecture. It seemed as if old buildings, like pornography today, required some redeeming social value to be acceptable. Two categories were worthy of notice —those buildings that had been inhabited by founding fathers and those where the detailing provided a suitable background for the antiques which were presumed to be the primary concern of the magazine's readers. Of the dozen or so articles published during the decade, one, in February, 1931, posing the question "Was Washington Born in a Cabin?" dealt with the somewhat dubious reconstruction of his birthplace, Wakefield; a second, in May, 1933, was devoted to Stratford, the ancestral home of the Lees. Three articles examining architectural detail tended to condone an all-too prevalent form of white collar vandalism. This was the practice, indulged in by museums as well as private individuals, of removing significant detailing from old buildings for installation elsewhere as a suitable background for antique furnishings. An article on fireplaces in December, 1931, was illustrated mainly with examples thus divorced from their original settings. A series in 1932, entitled "Styles in Early Paneling," was an excellent survey, but bore the subtitle "Notes for the Home-Builder."

These two strains, the worship of ancestors and the decorative, were gradually institutionalized in the form of two more or less regular magazine features. One bore the general heading of "History in Houses," the other, first "Antiques in Domestic Settings," and later, the somewhat less formal "Living with Antiques." At the same time, new approaches to American architecture were beginning to appear in *Antiques'* pages. G. Edwin Brumbaugh's "Medieval Construction at Ephrata," which is included in this selection, introduced the magazine's readers to the painstaking, documentary approach to restoration that had begun to be developed in the 1930s. A series of articles by Nina Fletcher Little, published in 1945, "On Dating New England Houses," summarized the application of the correlation of scholarly documentary, decorative and structural analysis to the study of American architecture of one region. With increasing frequency in the 1950s and 1960s and on into the 1970s *Antiques* opened its pages to a range of articles covering American architecture from varying points of view. Brumbaugh's article has been followed by others describing restoration, while more general problems (and sometimes triumphs) in historic preservation have been well-recorded, particularly in the years when Barbara Snow was a member of the magazine's staff. Architectural historians like Robert C. Smith and Clay Lancaster have contributed important articles on style and taste.

Over the years *Antiques* has assembled a remarkable body of material dealing with American architecture, in particular with domestic architecture. Its coverage of individual buildings has been of especial value. For while books on architecture tend to concentrate (often repetitiously) on either spectacular or highly typical examples of the buildings of a particular period, region or style, *Antiques* has often explored the less familiar. Those of us with some interest in American architecture can predict that Monticello will be in the pages of almost every general book on the subject. We are far less likely to run across "Thomas Jefferson's Other Home," Poplar Grove. Almost any publication on Victorian domestic architecture will deal with Lyndhurst. The pages of *Antiques* may introduce us not only to that romantic Gothic pile, but to the smaller, and in some ways more intact, variation on the theme, Roseland in West Woodstock, Connecticut. Not that *Antiques* has neglected the major monuments. It has examined Cliveden and the Van Cortlandt Manor House, Woodlawn and the Pepperell Mansion, Hyde Hall and Mount Pleasant, the Trent House and the Hermitage, in short, all the textbook examples. But it has given at least equal time to the less well-known and less accessible buildings, including many in private ownership. The roster includes a good number of "great houses" in the traditional sense, of plantations and estates set in rolling lawns and artful groves, and/or urban mansions. It has not, however, ignored the less pretentious structures that serve to illuminate the history of American building arts, of careful craftsmanship in wood and stone, whether executed by seventeenth-century New Englanders or nineteenth-century German and Scandinavian settlers in Wisconsin.

Perhaps the greatest strength in *Antiques'* coverage of American architecture lies in the lavish use of illustrations—not for *Antiques* the single view of the facade or a principal room. Most buildings are shown in loving detail, if not quite from cellar to attic, at least beyond the front hall and best parlor into dining rooms, bedrooms, libraries and even kitchens. The reader is given a far better opportunity than in most publications to comprehend the totality of a building's design and decor. The decor must not be forgotten. Great houses tend to contain great things and since this is, after all, *Antiques* and not *Architectural Record*, the illustrations, and the text, often dwell on the furnishings and their relationship to the interiors. A word of caution should be inserted here. Few houses in this country have remained in the condition in which they were built. Ownership changes, and styles in architecture, as well as in furnishings and their arrangement, shift with changing tastes. Most of the buildings shown here have undergone one or more changes, either to update them according to a new fashion or to strip away later alterations through restoration. What we see in these illustrations, then, is a view of the past, often highly accurate, but a view usually made at some specific later time and conditioned by the resources and knowledge then available. Thus the best restorations will continue to change, subtly or radically, as more information or perhaps better or more suitable furnishings become available. As a case in point, the interiors of the Peyton Randolph House in Williamsburg have been considerably refurbished since the article and accompanying illustrations reproduced here were published in January, 1969. Yet preservation of a photographic record of the rooms as they looked in the 1960s is in itself important. For we need to continue to evaluate our own changing knowledge of the past in terms of what our predecessors knew, to learn from their mistakes and emulate their successes.

The article on the Peyton Randolph House appeared in an issue devoted entirely to Colonial Williamsburg. Such special issues form another of *Antiques'* outstanding features. Some, like that on Williamsburg, have explored the country's "village" restorations, Sturbridge, Shelburne and Greenfield. Other entire issues have considered larger areas, the cities of Philadelphia and Charleston, the state of Tennessee, New England as interpreted through the many and varied properties of the Society for the Preservation of New England Antiquities. In addition to these special issues, *Antiques* has often run articles which, rather than concentrating on a single building, have examined a town or region. At their best these articles have served to meld the decorative arts and architecture into a coherent and vivid picture of the distinctive characteristics of a time and place.

Antiques' coverage of American architecture has therefore exhibited many strengths. It has also been characterized by some conspicuous gaps. One of these is geographic. Especially in the earlier years, the magazine's pages have been dominated by the eastern seaboard, particularly, in fact, by the states of Massachusetts, Connecticut, Pennsylvania, Virginia, Maryland and South Carolina. There is, of course, some justification for this. These were the half-dozen among the original colonies where considerable wealth was first accumulated and first employed in the purchase of fine accoutrements for a life style of some elegance. They are also the areas in which institutions have traditionally tended to foster the study of the past. Nevertheless, they are only part of the tale of the decorative arts in America, and the view of American taste and development becomes distorted when it reflects only their image. Fortunately *Antiques* has occasionally redressed the balance in forays beyond the Appalachians, to examine the remarkable wall paintings of a Texas inn or the classical adobes of Monterey.

A second weakness is chronological. For readers of *Antiques* it may sometimes seem as if American creativity had stopped with the Centennial, if not with the Civil War. The magazine clearly serves an audience more interested in historic flasks than in Avon bottles, in Derby figurines than in Boehm birds. Still, high quality in architecture and the decorative arts did not vanish in the puff of a steam engine after the mid-nineteenth century. Nevertheless one looks in vain through *Antiques* for information on Art Nouveau or the Arts and Crafts movement or Art Deco. It would be gratifying to see these more recent, but by now "antique" styles, receiving the same attention that is meted out to the craftsmanship of an earlier day.

To select a sampling from the gleanings of some fifty years is never an easy task. The special issues devoted to a single city or region are particularly interesting, but space obviously precludes inclusion of more than a fraction of their contents. No articles from the 1930s and few from the 1940s have been reprinted. The insights they provided—however important they were at the time the articles were written—have become commonplace, expanded in numerous readily available subsequent publications, or else superseded by later scholarship. What has been chosen, however, forms a representative sampling. Emphasis has been given to articles covering material not readily available elsewhere, and spanning as wide a range of types and geography as possible.

The selection includes buildings that deserve the adjective "great" for a number of reasons. Some might be measured by the oldest criterion Americans have applied to their own architecture, association with great men or important events. Here are the homes of Thomas Jefferson and Andrew Jackson, of Brigham Young and Nicholas Biddle. Some are the work of renowned craftsmen or architects, like Samuel McIntire's The Vale, or the Barstow Mansion, attributed to Minard Lafever. Some deserve to be called great because they are excellent examples of a style or type. Many of the buildings shown fulfill, in fact, more than one of these criteria. Cliveden, for instance, was built by Pennsylvania's Chief Justice Benjamin Chew, and played a notable role in the Battle of Germantown. With its pedimented projecting center pavilion, its urn-bedecked roof, and its stairhall screened from the entry by a Doric colonnade, it is one of the finest Georgian mansions of the Middle Colonies. The article shows it as it looked when still occupied, as it was for some two hundred years, by members of the Chew family. Since then, the house, with most of its remarkable furnishings intact, has become the property of the National Trust for Historic Preservation and is open to the public on a regular basis.

Many of the buildings shown here were created great; others had greatness thrust upon them by virtue of survival. Among these are the small vernacular houses built by various ethnic groups that surely contribute as much to our knowledge of the American past as do the mansions of the wealthy. Although the articles that follow by no means constitute a history of vernacular architecture, they do touch on several facets—the Swedish Hendrickson house in Delaware, a Rhode Island stone-ender, the small Dutch houses of Long Island and the Hudson Valley, the patterned brick houses of New Jersey, stone buildings along the National Road, log houses in Wisconsin—among others.

Consideration of these forms among the "great" houses of America is valid. Retention of some of our older structures has value on more than one level. For a number of years there has been a consensus that buildings of extraordinary historical significance or great beauty or great antiquity should be studied and preserved. We are now beginning to realize that structures other than public buildings and stately mansions are important and irreplaceable documents. Until the twentieth century, history was the *Word*, recounted and vivified through documents and the written text. It was, therefore, most often the history of those who left a written record, of the statesmen, intellectuals, military men and divines, whose actions and thoughts were transcribed. More recently, because both current events and history can be communicated through other media—photographs, tapes, the movies, television—we have become more aware of the message of the object. Written history is reenforced and expanded by the testimony of the mute artifacts which enrich the texture of the past. In concentrating on detailed studies of individual buildings and areas, *Antiques* has made a notable contribution to our knowledge and understanding of an important part of our cultural heritage.

Constance M. Greiff
Princeton, New Jersey
August 1973

The restoration of the Eleazer Arnold house

in Lincoln, Rhode Island

BY *ABBOTT LOWELL CUMMINGS*, Assistant director, *Society for the Preservation of New England Antiquities*

SIXTY YEARS AGO, when the restoration of old houses first became a serious study, very little was said about the importance of "documenting" the work of restoration as it went along—that is, recording information about the structural history of the building by means of photographs and sketches and carefully written descriptions. As a matter of fact, although there exists a set of some half-dozen progress photographs taken as early as 1896 when the John Quincy Adams Birthplace in Quincy, Massachusetts, was restored, the effort to record has never become standard practice. To William Sumner Appleton, founder of the Society for the Preservation of New England Antiquities, it was a matter of fundamental importance. He conceived of the Society from the start as a storehouse of knowledge about New England's architectural past, and for him the old house was always more a "document" than a "period piece." His concern sprang largely from a prophetic insight into the very nature of restoration work. While its fundamental aim is to bring back or re-create original appearances, by this same token the more correct the restoration the more difficult it becomes to tell where original material leaves off and new work begins. In other words, once the architect and carpenters have disappeared from the scene it is often impossible to find anyone who can explain on just what evidence such and such details of the restoration were based or whether, for example, old paneling is original to the restored house in which it is found or was brought in from some other old house.

Closely related is the question of how far the work of restoration should be carried, a question for which Mr. Appleton found a conservative answer. "What is left today can be changed tomorrow," he wrote in 1921, "whereas what is removed today can perhaps never be put back." On the other hand, the Society has been faced more than once with the problem of a building which was in some danger of collapsing into its own cellar. Thorough overhauling has been necessary, and with a wealth of structural evidence brought to light it has been hard indeed to resist cutting back through later (and often interesting) layers to expose the original condition.

This was true of the Society's seventeenth-century Eleazer Arnold house in Lincoln, Rhode Island, built about 1687, and found in 1950 to be in need of complete structural rehabilitation. In the course of repairs it was decided to eliminate the surviving trim of the later eighteenth and the nineteenth centuries and restore the original portion of the house to its seventeenth-century as-

pect, leaving intact, however, a separate eighteenth-century chimney stack and second-story additions to the lean-to at the rear. Every effort was made to discover and record not only what evidence the fabric of the house itself could reveal, but also what early photographs, descriptions, deeds, and probate records had to tell. The net result is a restoration whose every detail can be reasonably supported. And anyone disturbed about the elimination, for example, of a late eighteenth- or early nineteenth-century fireplace in the process of exposing the original wide opening can find at least a careful pictorial and written record of what was removed.

The Eleazer Arnold house is one which students have loved for its persistent puzzles, not all of which were entirely solved by laying bare nearly every scrap of structural evidence the house had to offer. As early as 1895 Norman M. Isham (in his *Early Rhode Island Houses*) was concerned about both the original plan and the window arrangement. From what he could then see of the structure he assumed that the house had originally been built, as the rear slope of the stone chimney indicates, as a two-story house with lean-to and with its present full length, providing for two rooms at the front on the ground floor and two rooms behind them in the lean-to. The roof had been finished with an impressive façade gable, the valley rafters of which remain in the attic (though not restored). Without having full knowledge of evidence concealed in the frame of the house, Mr. Isham suggested the possibility of single casement openings in the front or south wall. By the time his *Early American Houses* was published in 1928 he had had a chance to explore enough of the hidden frame to know that the pattern of original wall studs there confirmed his supposition about these windows.

Seven or eight years later, with very little more of the frame exposed for study than it had been for Mr. Isham, Henry W. Gardner and Frank Chouteau Brown advanced in the columns of *Pencil Points* (February 1935) a complicated theory of evolution according to which the house began as a one-room, one-and-a-half-story structure. This was the present southwest room or great hall, subsequently raised to a full two stories, to which was added the lean-to kitchen, whose wide fireplace was located in an extension of the great stone end wall. Finally, the plan was made complete with an addition to the east or right-hand end of the house in which a separate chimney was eventually constructed. These conclusions were based on certain convincing features, long visible, which Mr.

Exterior of the Eleazer Arnold house from the southeast, showing its later windows and door before the restoration of 1950-1952. *Photograph by Arthur C. Haskell.*

Exterior from the southeast, showing the house as restored to its seventeenth-century appearance, 1950-1952.

Isham had not taken into consideration, at least in print, though for the most part very few facts were cited in the article to support the theory.

Yet, interestingly enough, among the mass of evidence uncovered during the restoration work of 1950-1952 were found a number of details (of which these writers could have known nothing) which tend to confirm their argument. The wall between the front and rear main rooms, for example, revealed mortises for studs, a worn threshold of an outside door in its "sill," and a suspicious break in the masonry of the adjoining foundation wall, all of which suggested that this now inner partition had once been the exterior rear wall. Still, the picture was by no means entirely clear, and it would be impossible to prove on the basis of all the evidence uncovered that either Isham or Gardner and Brown were totally right in their reconstructions of the original plan of the house. Any growth which may have taken place before the ground plan assumed its present form was early indeed, and as much as possible of the conflicting evidence has been left exposed for students of the future to puzzle over.

Perhaps the most interesting discoveries made during the restoration of 1950-1952 were further bits of evidence as to the arrangement of the original seventeenth-century small windows, long since replaced with larger hung sash, and the wealth of finely molded vertical wall sheathing. The inner partitions of the second story were found for the most part intact under later lath and plaster, ornamented with typical seventeenth-century channel moldings. Similarly, in the great hall below enough boards were found to provide a reliable model for the restored molded sheathing of this room.

Exterior from the northwest, showing the original stone end and pilastered chimney. *Haskell photograph.*

Eleazer Arnold house, Lincoln, Rhode Island. Fireplace wall in the great hall, with later mantel as it appeared before the Society acquired the house in 1918.

Fireplace wall in the great hall photographed in the spring of 1920, during the first stages of restoring the original fireplace. The latest or third fireplace is built inside the opening of a second, the oven for which can be seen at the right. Above the oven and at the far right are revealed the heavy lintel and stone jamb of the original fireplace.

Fireplace wall in the great hall showing the original opening which was found intact behind the later fireplaces. Some patching of the masonry was necessary along the rear face at the right.

The matter of the windows was more complicated. The location of those in the front or south wall was, as noted, clearly vouched for in the pattern of the wall studs, while the matching openings in the story above, for lack of more exact evidence, are largely conjectural. The most exciting piece of window evidence was found in the second story of the east, or end, wall, where not only was the triple width indicated in the surviving studs, but the exact height and vertical location were determined by cuts in these same studs. Above in the attic another triple window was indicated by the spacing of the studs there.

The restored casements and later guillotine windows in the east end may never have existed side by side at the same moment in time as they do now, but they help to differentiate clearly between the early period of the front rooms and the later style of the northeast room at the rear with its eighteenth-century fireplace. In this way it has been possible to preserve some trace at least of the later generations who occupied this house and whose changes and additions, incidentally, were for the most part of a marked architectural simplicity. Numbering from Eleazer Arnold, the original builder, through a direct line of his descendants all bearing the name of Arnold, there had been but six owners until the house came as a bequest to the several Arnold heirs who in 1918 presented it to the Society.

It was inevitable that some of the structural timbers would have to be completely renewed if the house was to continue to stand. All such new wood was marked as a means of identification for those who will find similar repairs necessary in another century or two. Every effort was made as well, in accordance with a long-standing policy of the Society, to duplicate those members of the frame which had to be replaced. If, for instance, wrote Mr. Appleton in 1924 in connection with some repairs to the Arnold house at that time, "we take out an oak sill 6 x 7, handhewn, 12 feet long and with six mortice holes I like to put back exactly that identical thing, counting on my photographs, [and] the manuscript record in our files here . . . to tell any future investigator that this is not the original sill, always supposing he isn't able to recognize the difference on looking at it."

Wholly of new materials were the stairs winding up steeply in the closet-like corner at the left of the fireplace in the great hall. The masonry, however, had preserved a series of holes into which the supports for the original stairs had been fitted, allowing a very close approximation of what was once there. For some features, however, no such evidence was found and it was necessary to rely on sources of another sort altogether. When the house came to the Society, for example, there could be found no trace of ovens in either of the large fireplaces which filled the great stone end. When the original openings were first restored under Mr. Isham's direction in the early 1920's the remains of at least one oven opening were found, but this was thought to be a later intrusion. Yet both the visitor and student will always look for some indication in these great fireplaces of where the baking was done. It was of interest, then, to discover in an account of the house by a nineteenth-century writer a reference to the oven as formerly projecting like a bulbous blister from the masonry of the great stone end—an interesting form of construction not uncommon in the seventeenth century but of which only a bare handful of New England examples now remain. The removal of this feature at some rather remote time has left little or no trace—a startling reminder of the importance of documenting those changes which will inevitably occur in an old house through the years. No restoration, it would seem, can be flawless, but the carefully recorded restoration will have the double advantage of authentic interest for the visitor and value as a source of factual information for the student.

The great hall is shown here as restored and furnished in 1950-1952. The molded wall sheathing is based on evidence found in this room.

History in houses

BY JOHN D. KURTZ

The Hendrickson house in the Delaware Valley

THE EFFORTS of the Swedish government to establish settlements in America in the seventeenth century were neither large nor long-lasting, and have been overshadowed by those of England, France, Spain, and Holland. But in the Delaware Valley—the area of Pennsylvania, New Jersey, and Delaware drained by the Delaware River, where the Swedes landed and remained from 1638 until 1655—the era of Swedish colonization is a well-recognized part of America's history. Both politically and culturally it has been surprisingly well documented, considering its remoteness and the fact that the records of an unsuccessful enterprise often suffer severe loss. Ferreting out the old records both here and in Sweden has been in the main accomplished by a number of dedicated, nonprofessional historians and antiquarians.

Lately an old Swedish house in the Delaware Valley has been saved from destruction by removal to a new site on the grounds of Old Swedes Church in Wilmington, Delaware. The original section of this house was

The ground-floor room, or hall, in the original (1690) part of the Hendrickson house. The large oval gate-leg table is Swedish, c. 1700, and descended through generations of one Delaware Valley family. Believed to be Swedish too is the rush-seated stool by the fireplace, with odd trumpetlike legs. Pewter candlesticks and wide-rimmed chargers, a copper bed warmer with sausage-turned handle, andirons and spit rod of wrought iron, and copper cooking vessels are among the useful smaller objects, European and American, of the late seventeenth or early eighteenth century. *Photograph by Willard Stewart, Inc.*

The original part of the house has a double batten door, secured by a stout wooden bar. The chairs in this room represent English and American types from 1670 to 1720. Of New England origin are the Pilgrim spindle-backs and the early Queen Anne chair against the wall, one of a pair. Though the house had two stairways, both were sharply turned and enclosed; this one is new, added to comply with city building regulations. *Stewart photograph.*

The great fireplace on the ground floor is large enough to stand or sit in, and has a small window. Steep winding stairs rise beside it to the second floor. *Photograph by Sanborn Studio.*

built in 1690, not far from the bank of the Delaware River just north of the present city of Chester, Pennsylvania. A Swede named John Hendrickson (that is, John, son of Hendrick) had it constructed for his younger brother, Andrew, on the occasion of the latter's marriage to a girl named Brigitta, who is identified in the old records as "daughter of Morton."

Some time after 1798, the size of the house was increased by the addition of a stone section of the same height and depth as the original but roughly half its length. This newer part is identical with the older in general exterior construction, so that the house appears as a rectangular unit. This method of enlargement, as opposed to the addition of a wing or a lean-to, is not unusual for the region.

The Hendrickson house is one of the very few authenticated early Swedish houses extant in this country. It appears to have been occupied continuously as a dwelling until about 1925, when it was acquired by the Baldwin Locomotive Works. Fortunately, the Baldwin management recognized its historical significance, and not only took considerable pride in possessing the place, but was careful to see that it did not suffer further deterioration. By 1957 the structure had passed out of Baldwin ownership, however, and was scheduled for demolition to make room for expansion of the Vertol Aircraft plant. Realizing its historical value, this firm offered it to several local groups interested in preservation. Valiant efforts were made to raise enough money to move the house to Governor Printz Park in nearby Tinicum Township, but they were unsuccessful.

At this juncture, news of the matter came to the vicar of Old Swedes Church in Wilmington, which was built in 1698-1699 by the Swedish settlers. With no particular

funds available for such a project, but with great enthusiasm and confidence in its ability eventually and somehow to raise the substantial sum which would be involved, the Holy Trinity, Old Swedes, Church Foundation asked for and obtained possession of the house late in 1958. The old site was carefully explored, extensive photographs and measured drawings were made, and minute construction data were recorded before the house was taken apart. Amateurs were enlisted for a careful search for any artifacts about the site, under the guidance of an experienced professional archeologist; this

This small walnut *kas*, made in Delaware or Pennsylvania c. 1700, is unusual in having a single door. The well-turned William and Mary chair with cane back and leather seat is of fruit wood painted black, while the turned candlestand shows traces of old red paint. The wrought-iron candlestand is equipped with snuffers. *Stewart photograph.*

The large room on the second floor in the old part of the house has two grills of turned spindles in the paneling of the fireplace wall. The long pine trestle table, c. 1700, is believed to be Swedish. A painted Swedish sugar box stands on the pine two-drawer table, c. 1730. The Pennsylvania painted and inlaid cupboard dates from about 1760. *Stewart photograph.*

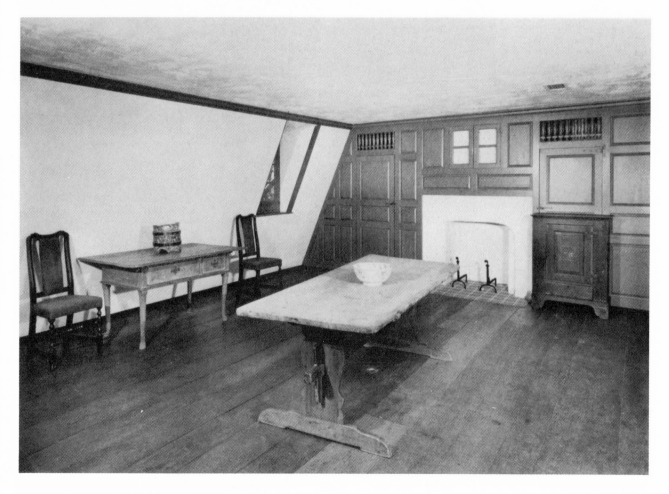

part of the project was most interesting but not correspondingly rewarding, as very little was found.

The house has now been re-erected at the southwesterly edge of the Old Swedes burial ground, to serve as a museum and church office (see frontispiece). Its exterior appearance is almost precisely what it must have been in the early days after the enlargement. However, through the years much of the woodwork, both outside and in, had deteriorated to such an extent that it could not be salvaged. The roof shakes, or shingles, and all the main timbers are new, but the shakes are hand-hewn and the timbers are hand-adzed, and they approximate very closely the old ones which they replace. Although not original to the house, the flooring and most of the paneling are appropriate in both age and type, having been obtained from approximately contemporary structures.

Some changes in the interior plan were necessary to adapt the building to its new function and to comply with building code regulations. The greatest of these changes is the placing of a stairway leading to the basement, where a vault for parish documents and other valuables is provided, and to the second floor, where a meeting room and an office are located. In the main ground-floor room, the large fireplace, which had been greatly reduced in size at some time during the years, has been restored to its original condition. It is of noteworthy dimensions, and contains a small window. Fortunately the well-molded mantel and surround had been left in place, though partly plastered over; these have now been uncovered and restored. The chimney lintel, which is original, is a massive oaken timber about eighteen inches square and eight feet long.

Furnishing this old house with anything like historic accuracy presented a considerable problem, since authentic seventeenth-century Swedish-American pieces are extremely scarce. However, many appropriate items have been acquired, and it is hoped that others may be added as opportunity—and funds—permit.

Descriptions of the furnishings in the captions to the pictures shown here are based on information supplied by David Stockwell.

The ground-floor room in the later part of the house has its own exterior door and one of the two original stairways, as well as fielded paneling on the fireplace wall. *Sanborn photograph.*

The small upper room in the later part of the house has sheathing on the end wall, and a door shutting off the steep stairway. *Sanborn photograph.*

The eighteenth-century house

in America

BY ROBERT C. SMITH

EIGHTEENTH-CENTURY HOUSES IN AMERICA were essentially a restatement, in our own terms, of English buildings of the period. This English architecture of the eighteenth century was by no means indigenous, but was the result of many influences of different origins and diverse expressions. The Palladianism of the Italian ideal and the practical application it had received from the Dutch; the rococo of France and its exotic Chinese affiliations; the new Romanism of Robert Adam, and the Greek spirit that came with the architecture of James "Athenian" Stuart—all were drawn together by a constantly increasing emphasis on classicism, the unifying keynote of the eighteenth century.

Each influence was reflected in this country, through the use of British pattern books, the coming of English architects, and the development of taste by means of European travel. As a result there grew up here an academic approach to architecture which is entirely different from the medieval vernacular of our seventeenth-century builders.

This point of view was first expressed at Williamsburg, Virginia, where the public buildings (1699-1732), as shown in the Bodleian plate, the chief authority for their restoration, all conform to one general pattern. Their neat rectangular façades with regularly spaced windows, central doors, and hipped roofs can be traced back to a model by the Italian architect Sebastiano Serlio, drawn before 1550 but not published until 1575, five years after similar designs by Palladio had appeared in print. In the seventeenth century it was the model for the Mauritshuis, constructed at The Hague in 1633 by Pieter Post on designs by Jacob van Campen. Minus the pediment and pilasters the style was introduced to England in Restoration houses like Eltham Lodge, built by Hugh May in Kent about 1668. When William and Mary came to London from Holland in 1689 this new version of the old Italian model became the basis for an intimate Anglo-Dutch style incorporating new sash windows in place of the old casement variety, which was introduced to Vir-

ginia following the work of Sir Christopher Wren at Kensington Palace and other official residences.

We call these buildings Queen Anne because they reached the height of their development in England during her reign, from 1702 to 1714. Although we had a few late seventeenth-century examples, the style was typified here by the Governor's Palace at Williamsburg, which was built in that period. It remained in favor through the first half of the eighteenth century; as late as the 1750's the Wythe house in Williamsburg and Carter's Grove near by on the James River were designed in this fashion.

Sometimes the closest stylistic connections can be found between English and American Queen Anne houses. The G. Momperson house, built in Salisbury, England, in 1704, is very similar to Stenton, erected for William Penn's secretary James Logan at Germantown, Pennsylvania, in 1728. The treatment of the pair of narrow windows flanking the main door in both houses is practically identical.

The interiors of houses of this sort give an impression of luxury and academic elegance that was new in British America. In our still medieval seventeenth-century dwellings, like the John Ward house built at Salem, Massachusetts, around 1685, the main rooms contain huge, utilitarian fireplaces, so high that a man can stand inside them. In the eighteenth century these survived in simple farmhouses, in country inns, and in mansion kitchens. In fine Queen Anne houses, on the contrary, fireplaces became much smaller and were treated as a part of continuous wall paneling of geometric form. Generally without mantel shelves, they were frequently decorated with prominent return moldings called crossettes, which again go back to Serlio. The fireplace was often set, on Anglo-Dutch precedent, in an angle of the room, so the chimney could serve two rooms per story, as at William Trent's house of 1719 in Trenton, New Jersey.

Along with the use of geometric paneling came the introduction of the classical orders by means of pilasters and entablatures. The earliest examples here, like the Doric pilasters in the hexagonal hall at Stenton, were

Design for the Villa Marocco (c. 1570) by Andrea Palladio. The British revival of the style made popular by this Renaissance architect was introduced to America by imported pattern books about the middle of the eighteenth century.

This article is a condensation of a talk given by the author at the 1954 Williamsburg Antiques Forum.

Land façade of Brandon in Virginia (c. 1765). Believed to have been designed by Thomas Jefferson, it follows closely the pattern books based on Palladio's writings. *Photograph by Flournoy.*

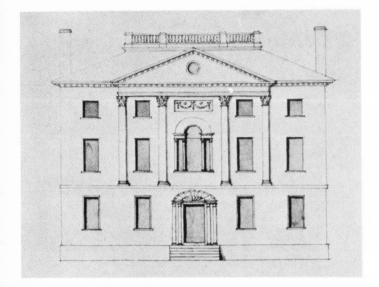

Design for the Joseph Coolidge house in Boston by Charles Bulfinch. This drawing for the residence built in 1792 and destroyed about 1843 is an early example of the influence of the Adam style in New England. *New York Public Library.*

Room from the Powel house, Philadelphia (c. 1768) now in the American Wing, Metropolitan Museum of Art. Close in spirit is the Chippendale furniture of Philadelphia and the Chinese painted paper, whose "boasted villas of Pekin" recall the vogue for chinoiserie decoration in garden houses of the second half of the eighteenth century. *Metropolitan Museum of Art.*

Parlor of the William Trent house built in Trenton, New Jersey, in 1719. The fireplace was set in the corner for increased efficiency following Anglo-Dutch precedent. *Photograph by Moyer.*

Dining room at Gore Place, Waltham, Massachusetts (c. 1800). Federal style at its best decorated in the manner of Robert Adam. *Ladies' Home Journal; photograph by Ezra Stoller.*

often inaccurately proportioned and crudely cut. In the Metropolitan Museum's pentagonal room from Marmion in Virginia, which is slightly later, the Ionic pilasters are much finer and probably reflect the greater academic learning among the builders and woodcarvers whose activity centered around Williamsburg. By the middle of the century fine fireplaces in all the colonial centers were generally framed by correctly carved pilasters and inset cupboards, like the beautiful examples made about 1750 for The Lindens, a Massachusetts house moved in recent years to Washington, D.C.

About this time Philadelphia became the colonial headquarters for a more elaborate kind of woodwork. This coincided with the introduction to this country in the 1740's of the eighteenth-century British revival of the style of Andrea Palladio, the great Renaissance architect of northern Italy whose dream had been to restore the grandeur and beauty of Roman building, as he conceived it. His plans were disseminated by dozens of pattern books imported from London. The State House in Philadelphia (Independence Hall) has our finest colonial example of the wood-carved Palladian interior, where a theatrical screen of Doric columns, pilasters, frieze, and cornice provides a majestic background for affairs of state. It became fashionable to imitate this academic *mise en scène* and small editions soon appeared in the Royall House at Medford, Massachusetts, rebuilt in 1747, and in Virginia at William Buckland's Gunston Hall (1755-1758) and the contemporary Pott's Grove in Pennsylvania.

British architects took from Palladio's writings the plan of the five-part house, consisting of a central residence block, united to terminal pavilions by passages which combine the beauty of varying proportions with the comfort of protection from bad weather. This scheme became popular in great plantation houses of Virginia and Maryland. At first the advance buildings were merely brought into line with the main block of the residence, as at

Westover (c. 1730) on the James, which is a regular Queen Anne mansion with an end pavilion modeled on the story-and-a-half advance buildings of the Governor's Palace at Williamsburg. In later examples like Brandon (c. 1765) the end pavilions are joined to the main block by Palladian passage wings and the façades are much closer to the Italianate norm of the pattern books. At Mount Vernon and Mount Airy, which are contemporary (1758), there are connecting passages which curve in a way Palladio illustrated.

In addition to pedimented door and window frames, another of the classical features derived from Palladio was the Roman temple portico. In his *Four Books of Architecture* there are designs for both single and double "piazzas," as they came to be called. The latter existed as early as the 1730's in South Carolina, where it offered relief from hot weather, and is represented in its most splendid form in the beautiful porch of the Miles Brewton house at Charleston, carved by Ezra Waite before 1769. Brandon may have had the same kind of portico.

The single or colossal variety is much rarer. One of the few authentic colonial examples is the one that dominates the river façade of White Hall, the house erected for Governor Sharp of Maryland near Annapolis about 1795. Attributed to young Thomas Jefferson, who is also given credit for designing Brandon, the temple front of White Hall was repeated constantly after the Revolution, and in the early nineteenth century was demonstrated in all the architectural orders at Jefferson's University of Virginia, our greatest monument to Palladio.

Colonial houses reached the climax of their development in the two golden decades before the Revolution. Characteristic of their exteriors is the use of a slightly

Design for a house (c. 1550) by Sebastiano Serlio, whose treatise on architecture served with that of Palladio as a model for seventeenth-century buildings in Holland and England. The style which developed appeared in America in the public buildings at Williamsburg, Virginia.

Bodleian plate. Engraved views of buildings at Williamsburg, Virginia, by an unknown artist, found in the Bodleian Library, Oxford. *Colonial Williamsburg, Inc.*

projecting pedimented section, which gives a new sense of depth to the rest of the building. Sometimes this was emphasized by the use of angle pilasters, as in the rare cut-stone façade of Chalkley Hall, built in 1776 at Frankford (Philadelphia) on the Delaware. By these architectural devices Serlio's old pattern was finally completely restated in America.

At the same time the curving fantasies of the French rococo began to appear in the interiors of these houses. In the Philadelphia Powel house room of about 1768, now at the Metropolitan, this is seen in the asymmetrical carving of the overmantel and other details of the woodwork, as well as in the delicate fluttering garlands of the plaster ceiling, which may have been executed by craftsmen like Gabriel Valois, who came to Philadelphia directly from France. It should be noted, however, that here, as in the great room at White Hall, where rococo masks ornament the cove of the plaster ceiling, these elements of fantasy are subordinated to the basic framework of the room, which is still Palladian in design. Colonial craftsmen found these rococo novelties, together with Gothic inventions, in the popular pattern books of Batty Langley, but they used them with a discretion which proves their real loyalty to the classic forms.

In 1761 the great English architect and interior decorator Robert Adam, fresh from archaeological researches in Rome, designed a series of state apartments for the Duke of Northumberland's Syon House outside London. The decoration, based in large measure on recent excavations at Herculaneum and Pompeii, provided a more literal evocation of ancient Roman art and turned the tide of taste, first in England, then in this country. Such grandiose effects as those of Syon House could not be attempted in America, for no one was rich enough to build on that scale here. But after the Revolution craftsmen soon excelled in a more modest use of the delicate ornament Robert Adam had developed, in rooms with curving walls patterned on those of antique Roman buildings.

New England became the center of this Federal style,

succeeding Philadelphia, as the latter had previously outstripped Virginia, especially in relation to the wood-carved interior. Charles Bulfinch, the architect of Boston, and Samuel McIntire, the architect-woodcarver of Salem, together developed the new squarer, box-like houses, surmounted by balustrades and decorated, both inside and out, with minute classical ornament, which are the outstanding architectural contribution of the age. The pattern books of Asher Benjamin, first published in 1797 at Greenfield, Massachusetts, carried these designs to the rest of the country and broke the old tradition of depending on England for plans. This did not, however, end the flow of architectural ideas across the Atlantic, for before the end of the century Benjamin Henry Latrobe had reached the shores of Virginia with the latest London formula for perfecting the classical ideal, by imitating Greek architecture instead of Roman.

Thus, in five phases eighteenth-century American craftsmen followed the academic pathway from Serlio and Palladio back to Athens and Pompeii, and the American house underwent successive changes, almost decade by decade, which made it appear constantly more classical. Through the whole period certain regional differences, both general and specific, can be found. The architects of New England frequently preferred wood, while those of Virginia favored brick, and much of the fine building of the middle Colonies was in stone. Similarly, the stairs of Virginia houses are noted for their Renaissance ornament, those of Massachusetts for their baroque spiral bannisters, and those of Philadelphia for occasional rococo brackets. The Federal woodcarvers of the Delaware River area developed a unique system of decorating their mantels, cornices, and door frames by gouging and punching tiny shields, stars, urns, and garlands, of Hepplewhite design. In spite of these differences, however, all our centers of production maintained the same high standards of craftsmanship and taste which make their work one of the great accomplishments of the eighteenth century in art.

The Peyton Randolph House

The Peyton Randolph House faces the Market Square. Noteworthy architectural features are the hooded front entrance and the wooden belt board at the second-floor line.

The impressive — and unorthodox — character of the Peyton Randolph House is more apparent from the rear than from the front. Here one sees the original structure, built perhaps as early as 1715, at the right, and in the center the post-1724 addition, where the tall arched window lights the great stairway shown on the frontispiece. These two-story sections contain the present exhibition rooms; the lower wing at left is a reconstruction and not open to view.

THE HOUSE OF ONE of Williamsburg's most distinguished citizens in the eighteenth century, Peyton Randolph (c. 1721-1775), is one of the most distinguished of Colonial Williamsburg's exhibition buildings today, and in some ways the most interesting. The elongated building with its many architectural merits grew to its present size over a period of years: Sir John Randolph, Peyton's father, first occupied the westernmost section, which may be as early as 1715, then in 1724 acquired a story-and-a-half house next door. Later, the middle two-story section was built to join the two together. Within the house is a remarkable series of original paneled rooms, and they have been furnished as handsomely as they deserve.

Peyton Randolph was one of the great statesmen of colonial America. After attending the College of William and Mary and being trained for the law in London, he devoted his life to public service, a representative of the conservative colonial aristocracy yet a leader of the patriot cause. He served as King's attorney, chairman of the Virginia committee of correspondence, speaker of the House of Burgesses for the ten years before the Revolution, and first president of the Continental Congress.

After his death the house continued to be occupied by his widow, the former Elizabeth Harrison, daughter of Colonel Benjamin Harrison IV of Berkeley and sister of Benjamin Harrison the Signer. On her death in 1783 it passed out of the family, and Colonial Williamsburg acquired it in 1938.

Peyton Randolph's study is in the oldest part of the house. The theme of baroque curves and scrolls —the leitmotif of the first half of the eighteenth century—is played with fascinating variations in this room, especially in the doors and double arch of the English oak desk-and-bookcase, the crest of the English burl-walnut looking glass, the contours of the New England walnut easy chair, and the shape of the window valances, which were fashioned of eighteenth-century red wool moreen after a pattern in the Williamsburg collection. The "Desk & Book case" listed in Randolph's inventory of 1776 is the documentation for placing one here; the useful litter on it includes an equinoctial dial from Augsburg, c. 1770, and a magnifying glass from London, 1771-2. Books fill the shelves of the hexagonal library table (shown in the article on the English furniture) and of the large English mahogany bookcase with glazed doors, c. 1760, which represents one of "6 Mahogany Book Presses" listed in the inventory. Peyton Randolph inherited his father's library and on his own death it was bought by his cousin Thomas Jefferson, whose library in turn became the nucleus of the Library of Congress. A view of the fireplace corner of this room is shown with *The maps and pictures.*

The dining room in the Peyton Randolph House is virtually a cabinet of choice English silver and porcelain. On the George II octagonal walnut table, a set of four silver candlesticks by David Green (London, 1723-4) surrounds a flat-chased punch bowl by Richard Gurney and Thomas Cook (London, 1739-40), which in turn rests on the dish cross shown in the article on the silver. Also shown there are several of the pieces on the American mahogany sideboard table, and on the English shelves above. The tureen on the table is Bow porcelain, c. 1755, and the porcelain on the shelves, mostly Chelsea, has decorations or forms taken from nature—shells, birds, and plants; a pair of shell salts on the bottom shelf was made at Bow, c. 1755. The nature motif is repeated in the large flower painting, probably Dutch, c. 1700, above the fireplace. Three soft-paste porcelain figures adorn the mantel: those at left and right are from the Girl-in-a-swing factory, London, c. 1750; that in the center is Derby, c. 1755. The slip covers of the Massachusetts Queen Anne chairs are of eighteenth-century silk bourette, the same material that lines the window curtains in this room,

For other illustrations, see color insert.

A comfortable easy chair and a variety of small useful objects give an intimate air to the corner chamber of the Peyton Randolph House. On the bedside table and chest of drawers are a tape loom, a wig stand, a wig-powdering carrot, a beadwork casket, an embroidered pocketbook, a snuffbox of horn, and a shoehorn of steel. Framed engravings brighten the wall: *Poetry, Astronomy,* and *Painting,* from a set of five *Arts and Sciences* published in London c. 1755. The bedstead, of mahogany throughout, is believed to have been made in Newport c. 1780. It is hung with a copperplate-printed English chintz shown in detail with the textiles; the bedspread, probably French, c. 1750-1780, is of moire and has its original knotted fringe.

While most of the paneling in the Peyton Randolph House is of the customary yellow pine, this bedroom on the second floor of the oldest part of the house is paneled entirely in oak. The rich, mellow color is a foil to the brilliant blue and white flame pattern of the bedspread and window curtains, of an antique tie-dyed cotton fabric. The dressing table here is a Maryland piece, c. 1760, of walnut with Southern yellow pine and white cedar. The mahogany side chair, one of a pair, is also from Maryland, while the walnut corner chair, c. 1740, is from New England. Slightly earlier is the handsome English dressing glass, of walnut veneer on oak, with gilding. Partially visible in the closet beyond are the English bidet shown in *The English furniture,* and an American candlestand, c. 1730, of iron and brass.

BY ALICE WINCHESTER

Living with antiques

Cliveden, the Germantown home of Mr. and Mrs. Samuel Chew

IN THIS RESTLESS nation of ours, ancestral homes that have always been lived in by one family are remarkably rare. Our tradition has been for the rising generation to leave home—often to move westward—so that time and again our handsome early houses have passed into alien hands and fallen into disrepair, eventually to be demolished completely or perhaps to be rescued belatedly at the cost of extensive restoration. One of the happy exceptions to this rule is Cliveden, the seat of the Chew family in Philadelphia's Germantown. Since 1761 when it was built the house has remained continuously in the family, except for an eighteen-year interval at the close of the eighteenth century, and it is now occupied by the sixth generation of direct descendants of the original owner, Benjamin Chew.

Benjamin Chew (1722-1810), trained for the bar in Philadelphia and London and holder of various public offices in Delaware and Pennsylvania, is known to history as an eminent jurist. From 1774 until the outbreak of the Revolution he was chief justice of the supreme court of Pennsylvania and from 1791 to 1808, judge and president of the high court of errors and appeals of Pennsylvania. In 1777, with his friend Governor John Penn, he was temporarily "enlarged upon parole" in "the back country" of New Jersey because his patriotism was considered in doubt; in fact, however, his sympathies were

fundamentally with the American cause, and less than a year later he was permitted to return to Philadelphia. He is considered one of the significant figures of our late colonial and early Federal period.

Benjamin Chew was married twice, first to his cousin Mary Galloway who died in 1755, then two years later to Elizabeth Oswald, who became the mother of his first son, Benjamin Jr. One of his daughters was Peggy, a celebrated beauty, who was courted by Major André and later married Colonel John Eager Howard of Maryland. A portrait of the latter hangs at Cliveden, and poems written by the ill-fated major to Peggy Chew are preserved there.

For much of his life, Chew maintained a residence in Philadelphia. Cliveden was built as his summer home, on a site north of old Germantown which was added to gradually until it comprised sixty acres. The handsome house was set well back from the road, sheltered by trees and shrubbery and accented by marble statuary placed on the lawn. Chew named his estate for the famous English country seat of Frederick Louis, Prince of Wales, where the latter had died and where his son, George III, grew up.

The American Cliveden was known then, as it is still, as one of the finest houses near Philadelphia. The Chew family spent much of each year there, and it was visited

Cliveden, built in 1761, is a dignified interpretation of English styles, combining classical details of Georgian character with the general proportions (except for the roof) of the Queen Anne manor house. The façade is of ashlar in gray Germantown stone, the sides and back are stuccoed. The columned doorway has a handsome pediment whose classic motifs are repeated in the cornice, and tall chimney stacks rise above the roof. Behind are two outbuildings, miniatures of the house itself; the one seen here, originally the kitchen, is connected to the house by a curved covered passage.

by many of the great of the day. But it met with disaster during the Revolution. In the battle of Germantown on October 4, 1777, it was the scene of heavy fighting; the house was riddled with bullets, woodwork and stonework were shattered, one cannon ball went straight through the house from front to back. The place was wrecked though not ruined, and Chew, who could not obtain materials for repairing it, sold it to a prosperous merchant named Blair McClenachan in 1779. In 1797 he bought it back, and the Chews have owned it ever since.

The successive generations that have lived at Cliveden have preserved not only the house but also its contents. Many pieces of eighteenth-century furniture which must have been acquired by Chief Justice Chew are still in place, some of them outstanding examples of Philadelphia craftsmanship. There are also numerous pieces of furniture as well as fireplace equipment and decorative objects in the neoclassic style of the Federal period, which were apparently added in the early 1800's: quite probably the house was refurbished by Benjamin Chew Jr. after his father's death in 1810. And, as in any house that is continuously lived in, later things too were added through the nineteenth century—pictures, china, furniture, ornaments of various kinds.

But nothing, apparently, was ever thrown away. When the present owner moved into the house last summer it was full of the accretions of the years, lovingly cherished by the last occupant, his nonagenarian aunt, Miss Elizabeth B. Chew, who had spent her life at Cliveden. Family papers and memorabilia of all sorts crammed attic, cellar, and outbuildings, while furnishings spanning nearly two hundred years were mingled throughout the house. Mr. and Mrs. Samuel Chew are still sifting through some of these precious possessions, but from the major rooms they have eliminated the pieces least appropriate to their setting. Now, its interior freshly painted and rearranged to suit today's pattern of living, its exterior little changed and carefully tended, Cliveden has taken a new lease on life as one of America's important historic houses.

At either side of the broad front hall is a handsome doorway; perhaps the small pedestal within the broken pediment originally supported a carving or piece of statuary. The room at the right of the hall has always been traditionally Mrs. Chew's sitting room, and that at the left (seen here), Mr. Chew's library. Today one wall of this room is lined with eighteenth-century leather-bound books that belonged to Chief Justice Chew. The Pennsylvania walnut desk has a handsome interior with tiered, shaped drawers. Above it hangs an attractive nineteenth-century primitive portrait of Cliveden.

The artist E. L. Henry (1841-1919), painter of genre, landscape, and portraits, reconstructed the 1777 battle of Germantown in this painting which hangs at Cliveden. While it is hardly a document, since it was painted long after the event, it is probably reasonably accurate and at any rate is a graphic story-telling picture. The statues spaced about the lawn, as well as the lions couchant flanking the door and the urns on the roof, are elegant features unusual for American houses. *Photographs by Charles P. Mills & Son.*

In design and detail, the hall at Cliveden is unusual if not unique in American domestic architecture. The entrance door, from which one views it here, faces four columns which virtually form a screen separating the broad expanse in front from the stair hall. The columns and their entablature repeat the classic details of the front door. The two Sheraton fancy chairs in the foreground are from a set of six in the house, painted dark green and red with gilding. The portrait at the right is of Benjamin Chew's sister-in-law, Peggy Oswald; that at the left, attributed to John Smibert, is his second wife's uncle and Chew's friend, Captain Joseph Turner. Memorabilia displayed in the vitrine below include Chew's seal and watch, a chatelaine he gave his wife, and bullets found at Cliveden after the battle of Germantown. Other reminders of the battle are the muskets leaning against a column, and round scars made in the floor beside them by the smoking barrels of firearms.

When the Marquis de Lafayette visited America in 1824 and 1825 he was entertained at Cliveden. Years later E. L. Henry depicted the scene as it must have appeared—the aging Frenchman shaking hands with everyone, the other guests bedecked in their best finery, an old veteran toward the right reminiscing, a lady at the left resting (and bored) after all the excitement, and in the rear hall uplifted hands bearing a laden tray of refreshments from the dining room. Apparently most of the furniture has been moved out of the hall for this reception, but the portraits of Turner and Peggy Oswald hang where they are today.

The drawing room is large and well-proportioned, with high ceiling, dentiled cornice, molded chair rail, and an imposing fireplace, mantel, and chimney breast. The two elegant Philadelphia mirrors are *en suite* with two large rectangular looking glasses in the room, all elaborately carved and painted white, to contrast with the blue of the walls. The matching card tables below and the fireplace equipment are part of a considerable group of nineteenth-century neoclassic furnishings in the house, probably acquired about 1810-1815.

The most distinguished piece of furniture in the house is the great sofa in the drawing room with boldly sweeping back and arms, Marlborough legs, and broad gadrooned skirt; legs, feet, and skirt are all ornamented with "gothic" carving (Hornor, *Blue Book of Philadelphia Furniture*, p. 151, Pl. 258). This piece was originally owned by Governor John Penn, for whom it was made by Thomas Affleck. Also made by Affleck for Penn between 1763 and 1766 and acquired from him by Benjamin Chew were the two upholstered side chairs or back stools here (Hornor, Pl. 262); they belong to a remarkable set of nine at Cliveden. A chair similar but lacking the fretwork corner brackets is at Winterthur (Downs, *American Furniture*, No. 163). The pair of Hepplewhite armchairs, painted white and gilded, recalls the painted beechwood chairs which Elias Hasket Derby of Salem ordered from Philadelphia in 1796 (Karolik collection, Hipkiss, Nos. 104, 105). The splendid mirror is one of a pair in the room, matching the two on the fireplace wall (Hornor, Pl. 439). The gilded griffon between the windows may originally have supported a marble slab. This carving belongs to the 1810-1815 period, as do the gilt wall brackets and the bronze and cut-glass Argand lamps with their original glass chimneys, and the neoclassic card table and sewing table.

The dining-room walls, curtains, and seat cushions are a subtle hue between rose and gold that matches the border of a large set of French porcelain displayed in a cabinet in the room. Sheraton chairs painted brown and bronze with gilding are used with the three-part Hepplewhite mahogany table. The imposing chest of drawers is the work of Jonathan Gostelowe and bears his label in the top drawer (Hornor, Pls. 107, 108). The portrait above it is of Anne Sophia Penn Chew (c. 1860). The portrait of Benjamin Chew between the windows was painted by James R. Lambdin about 1872, after a silhouette done from life.

A Philadelphia double chest stands in the broad upper hall (Hornor, Pl. 139), a substantial piece with excellent detail in the fretwork frieze, dentiled cornice, and in the latticework and carved rosettes of the boldly scrolled pediment.

In Mrs. Chew's sitting room off the entrance hall stands a fine Philadelphia mahogany secretary which is distinguished by the carved bust in its pediment (Hornor, p. 119, Pl. 186), though efforts to identify the subject have thus far been unavailing.

History in houses

BY ROBERT L. RALEY

Hampton in Baltimore County, Maryland

The exterior of Hampton does not indicate its true size: the scale of windows, cornice, chimneys, and cupola makes the house appear much smaller than it is. Construction of the mansion was begun in 1783. A bill of "JEHU HOWELL, deceased, for doing part of Carpenters and Joyners work" (in possession of the Maryland Historical Society), includes the listing of "28 feet of hand-Railes with Chenie-work" at five shillings per foot. The wing at the right was used as a farm office and laundry. *Photograph by the author.*

Water-color view of Hampton, c. 1850. Comparison with the mansion today reveals that the exterior has remained almost unchanged. *Maryland Historical Society.*

From north to south through the center of the main block of Hampton runs the great hall, measuring 53 by 22 feet. Henry Thompson of Clifton noted that when fifty-one guests sat down here to dinner, "everyone had plenty of room" (manuscript diary in the possession of the Maryland Historical Society). In the center of the floor is a large Sarouk rug, and on the wall opposite the stair-hall door hangs a classical Italian landscape brought back by Eliza Ridgely (1803-1867) from one of her European tours. The small window seat at the extreme right end of the hall is one of a pair which formerly belonged to Betsy Patterson, the Baltimore beauty who married Napoleon's brother Jerome. All of the mirrors are original to the house; the Waterford chandeliers are a recent gift.

Except as noted, photographs by Lanny Miyamoto.

Of all the great houses in America, Hampton perhaps has the most complete documentation. For over one hundred and fifty years it remained the home of the Ridgely family, and in it were preserved all of the documents relating to its construction. Only recently these records were presented to the Maryland Historical Society by Mr. and Mrs. John Ridgely, the last occupants.

Robert Ridgely, the first of this family in America, migrated from England to St. Mary's County, Maryland, in the seventeenth century. His grandson Charles, "the merchant," acquired Northampton, a fifteen-hundred-acre tract of land in Baltimore County. Within a few years he had enlarged the estate, by additional purchases, to over seven thousand acres. When Charles Ridgely died in 1772 his will confirmed a 1760 grant of two thousand of these acres to his son, another Charles, who was to be known as "the builder." Construction of Hampton was begun by this Charles Ridgely in 1783, and it took seven years to complete. It was largely financed by the profits of the Ridgely iron furnaces.

Unfortunately Charles the builder did not live to enjoy his new home, for he died in 1790 within six months of its completion. Childless, he left his wife Rebecca a life interest in "the Dwelling wherein I now reside" or, if she preferred, "the new house I am now building, I leave it at her option to Choose the same." Rebecca Ridgely wanted neither; she chose another estate, where she lived until her death in 1812. By the provi-

sions of Ridgely's will a nephew, Charles Ridgely Carnan, then inherited his uncle's house and a large part of the land. To meet the will's requirements, Carnan assumed Ridgely as surname: as Charles Carnan Ridgely he served as governor of Maryland from 1816 to 1819. He is remembered in contemporary accounts as a "genteel man" noted for his hospitality.

The identity of Hampton's designer is not positively known, but it may well have been Jehu Howell, who was referred to in a Baltimore newspaper of 1787 as a "very ingenious architect." In the Ridgely papers there is a bill rendered by the estate of Howell for £3,482.13.6½ for carpentry and woodwork (William B. Hoyt Jr. has published these accounts in the *Maryland Historical Magazine* for December 1938, pp. 352-371). A comparison of the paneling installed in the first- and second-floor rooms is interesting. Howell was responsible for the finishing of the second floor, and after his sudden death in 1787 the first-floor woodwork was finished in a plainer but more contemporary style.

As it stands today, Hampton is an imposing late-eighteenth-century American house almost purely Palladian in design. Its plan, with dominating central hall and subordinate stair, follows the Palladian precepts that were still being observed in England by such architects as Robert Pain and Sir William Chambers. The symmetry of the main block and identical wings is as typical of the Palladian school as are the great porticoes. If

At the south end of the great hall hangs a copy of Sully's portrait of Eliza Ridgely. The daughter of Baltimore merchant Nicholas Greenberry Ridgely, Eliza came to Hampton as the bride of John Ridgely, son of Governor Charles Ridgely. The original of this famous *Lady with the Harp* is now in the National Gallery of Art in Washington. The pianoforte below the portrait, made by H. Kisting, "Pianofortemaker of the Royal Court of Berlin," and sold by F. A. Wagler of Washington, was originally purchased for Emily Machen of Walney, Fairfax County, Virginia. The book of music belonged to Eliza Ridgely and bears her initials.

Although the harp in the music room is not the one shown in Sully's portrait, it was purchased by Eliza Ridgely's father from "Sebastian Erard, Inventor of the Harp" in London in June 1817. The original bill for this instrument (it had "silver strings" and cost £ 110.14) is in the collection of the Maryland Historical Society. On the floor is an Aubusson carpet in shades of rose. The tilt-top table is set with a white and gold grisaille Sèvres tea service. Only the corner of the handsomely curved and inlaid Baltimore sofa can be seen. This piece was presented to Hampton by the Maryland Chapter I of the Colonial Dames of America, who are responsible for the furnishings of the room. Above the inlaid and painted mahogany pianoforte, made by Joseph Hisky of Baltimore (c. 1830), is a portrait of Mary II of England, complemented by a strong study of the Duke of Wellington over the fireplace. The crystal chandelier is original to the room and was probably installed during the residency of the governor or his son John.

the new republic can be symbolized in terms of architecture, there are few places where it is as completely and expressively represented as in the development of these loggias. Palladio's own view on porches is significant: "Vitruvius says [in the first and sixth books] for the great men and particularly those in a Republic, the houses are required with loggias and spacious halls adorned, that in such places those may be amused with pleasure, who shall await the master . . ."

In May 1948, Hampton was designated a national historical site. The house and forty-five acres of land surrounding it were purchased by the Avalon Trust Foundation, founded by Mrs. Ailsa Mellon Bruce. Additional funds were granted by the foundation for the restoration of the house and for the purchase of part of the original furnishings. Mr. and Mrs. John Ridgely, the former owners, have presented many of the family portraits now hanging in the building.

Although not a great deal of restoration was needed, exterior walls were patched and painted and some of the woodwork repaired; the cupola was painted white, and the trim, the original buff. Inside, extensive studies were made to determine the colors first used. Wainscoting, cornices, and trim were repaired or duplicated, following original models.

The intention of the Society for the Preservation of Maryland Antiquities, custodians of the building, has been to restore the house and grounds to their appearance during Governor Charles Ridgely's occupancy. Hampton is now open to the public, except on Mondays.

Following the death of Governor Ridgely, the furnishings of Hampton were sold at auction. Undoubtedly John Ridgely and his wife Eliza, wealthy in her own right, bought back some of the more important family pieces. It is obvious from the furnishings of the drawing room that the young couple were also well aware of current European styles and wished to furnish some rooms of their new home in the latest taste. The rug is an Aubusson, of the same period as the set of decorated furniture, by tradition attributed to Phyfe, which descended through the Ridgely family. The gilt-gesso wall brackets and several pairs of mirrors hanging throughout the house are also family pieces. In the corner is a bust of the later Charles Ridgely who was master of Hampton from 1867 to 1872.

The woodwork in the dining room is the most elaborate on the first floor. The large, two-part dining table, although not original to the house, may well be like that listed in Ridgely's inventory as "1 Set Claw foot dining tables" valued at sixty dollars. Above the mahogany veneered and inlaid sideboard is a portrait of Charles Ridgely the builder by John Hesselius (1728-1778). In front of the windows stands a pair of shield-back chairs, similar to those used by William Hammond Dorsey (1764-1818) at his Georgetown home, The Oaks. To the left is a Sheraton serving table, one of the many Ridgely family pieces remaining in the house. The elaborate crystal chandelier formerly hung in the center of the great hall.

Indicative of the magnificent quality of Baltimore cabinetwork during the early years of the new republic is this superb wardrobe veneered in ebony, satinwood, and zebrawood, on loan from the Maryland Historical Society. Exhibited in 1947 at the Baltimore Museum of Art, this piece is illustrated (No. 89) in *Baltimore Furniture 1760-1810*, the catalogue of that show. To the right of the door is a portrait of James Howard (c. 1820), son-in-law of Governor Charles Ridgely. The carpet, matching that in the north bedroom, was ordered by Eliza Ridgely in Paris, as was the French crystal chandelier, which originally hung on the first floor.

This view of the north bedroom gives some idea of the great scale of the rooms. The deep rose and blue shades of the Turkey carpet set off the blue woodwork and white walls. To the left of the silk-upholstered Martha Washington chair are a blue and white China Trade porcelain tub and baby bath. A portrait of Eliza's husband, John Ridgely (1829-1867), hangs above the fireplace. The ornate chandelier was at Hampton when the mansion became a house museum.

Poplar Forest, Thomas Jefferson's "pleasant retreat," as it appears today.

Thomas Jefferson's other home

BY LUCILLE McWANE WATSON

ALTHOUGH MONTICELLO is viewed by increasing thousands of visitors throughout the year, Poplar Forest, the Bedford County plantation ninety miles away that Thomas Jefferson used as a "pleasant retreat" and that he himself considered "inferior only to Monticello," is virtually unknown outside its own Piedmont section of Virginia.

This obscurity is not accidental: Jefferson himself wanted it that way, and succeeding owners have kept it so. At the height of Jefferson's popularity as many as fifty guests at a time strained his purse and the hospitality of Monticello, and when the pressure of so many visitors became a burden, Poplar Forest provided the relaxation its owner required and the country pleasures in which he took such keen delight. Only to his intimates did he mention that it existed, and only a chosen few shared its enjoyments.

As he had done at Monticello and was later to do at the University of Virginia, Jefferson showed himself a disciple of the Italian classicist Andrea Palladio in his design for Poplar Forest. However, exactly how it looked when it was finished must be a matter of conjecture. The only known early picture of it, and that representing it before the addition of the "wing of offices," is a drawing done by Cornelia Randolph, Jefferson's granddaughter, about 1820. On November 6, 1845, the shingle roof of the house caught fire and was completely burned away. The interior woodwork also was destroyed. Today's roof, with dormer windows, was put on in the rebuilding im-

mediately following the fire. The walls, chimneys, and columns were unharmed and stand unaltered. Complete restoration for purposes of display has never been attempted, but the original character of the house has changed very little, and its rural setting remains unmarred. Farming goes on there today as in the beginning, and more than a thousand acres of the original tract still guard its traditional privacy.

Frequent references to Poplar Forest in Jefferson's garden book, his farm book, and his account book, as well as in his correspondence, show the painstaking efforts that went into the structure. Equally painstaking are notations on plantings there of trees, shrubs, and flowers, as well as of crops. When these notes from widely scattered collections are brought together there emerges a much clearer picture of Poplar Forest and its importance than could be viewed before; far from being merely a simple country home visited occasionally for rustic outings, the Bedford establishment was a year-around operation carefully directed in all its phases. The house that in time became its crowning glory was an architectural gem set in a beautifully ordered park, the gardens and surrounding fields blossomed at the hands of an expert horticulturist whose heart was in his plantings. The servants were given on-the-job training in the skills required for their assigned duties, and were provided with the best care and consideration. Products of its herds, mills, dairies, looms, and orchards were processed to meet the highest standards of the day. Best of all, its good neighbors and its tranquillity afforded one of the world's great masterminds "surcease from sorrow" and, after turbulent years, a measure of peace.

To his long-time friend, Dr. Benjamin Rush, signer of the Declaration of Independence and founder of the American Philosophical Society, Jefferson sent an oft-quoted observation that may well have been inspired in part by his friends of the Poplar Forest neighborhood. "I find friendships to be like wine, raw when new, ripened with age, the true old man's milk and restorative cordial." The same letter, dated August 17, 1811, and thus written when Jefferson was sixty-eight, tells of his great satisfaction with life there. "I write you from a place ninety miles from Monticello, near the New London of this state, which I visit three or four times a year and stay for a fortnight to a month at a time. I have fixed myself comfortably, keep some books here, bring others occasionally, am in a solitude of a hermit, and quite at leisure to attend to my absent friends."

Writing from Poplar Forest that same summer to Charles Willson Peale, another valued friend, Jefferson put down for posterity still more evidence of the joy the place afforded him. "I have often thought that if heaven had given me the choice of my position and calling, it would have been on a rich spot of earth, well watered and near a good market for the production of the garden. No occupation is so delightful to me as the culture of the earth, and no culture comparable to that of the garden . . . though I am an old man, I am but a young gardener." To the same correspondent Jefferson later wrote that "the plough is to the farmer what the wand is to the sorcerer."

Ten years later Jefferson's enthusiasm for his "Bedford abode" was unabated. On November 24, 1821, he wrote William Short, his former Albemarle neighbor and intimate, diplomat, secretary to the Paris legation, and later minister to Spain: "Your welcome favor of the 12th came to hand two days ago. I was just returned from Poplar Forest, which I have visited four times this year. I have an excellent house there, inferior only to Monticello, am comfortably fixed, and attended, have a few good neighbors, and pass my time there in a tranquility and retirement much adapted to my age and indolence."

It was through his wife that the original Bedford County tract of 4,819 acres had come into Jefferson's possession. By the death of her father, John Wayles, in 1773, Mrs. Jefferson had inherited in all some forty thousand acres and 135 slaves. The new owner's first recorded trip there was on September 8, 1773, and there are several references to other visits after 1779. Its seclusion was especially desirable in 1781, when Jefferson stayed there after the unsuccessful attempt of the British raider Tarleton to capture him at Monticello (he was governor of Virginia at the time). Taking his family with him to his "possession in Bedford," he remained long enough to recuperate from a fall from a horse soon after reaching three in June. Putting his enforced idleness to good account, he assembled the memoranda for his *Notes on Virginia*, completed in 1782 and later published in France. Thus it was that at Poplar Forest was written his only full-length book, "regarded today as the best statement of Jefferson's principles, the best reflection of

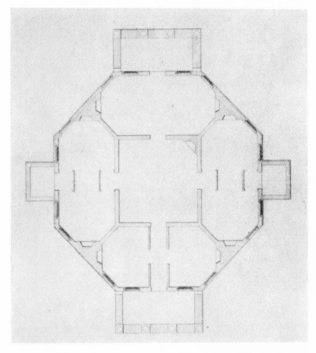

Floor plan of Poplar Forest.
Alderman Library,
University of Virginia.

Front elevation of Poplar Forest, drawn by Jefferson's granddaughter Cornelia Randolph about 1820.
Alderman Library,
University of Virginia.

his wide-ranging tastes and talents," according to the preface of the recent re-issue.

An "ample old-fashioned house" is said to have been the Bedford dwelling of those days. It was not until his second term as President that plans for the present building took shape.

After the death of his beloved wife, in 1782, Jefferson lavished his affections upon his daughters Martha and Maria, the only two of their six children who lived to reach womanhood. Martha, the eldest, became mistress of Monticello after her marriage to Thomas Mann Randolph in 1790. For the younger daughter, Maria, who married John Wayles Eppes, he planned a house to be built at Pantops, another of his farms in Albemarle. Maria's death in 1804, just after the foundations were begun, put an end to the project. It was this house originally designed for Pantops that Jefferson eventually built, with some changes, at Poplar Forest. It was started in 1806 and work on it continued at least as late as 1819.

On August 25, 1815, Mr. Jefferson wrote to the Reverend Charles Clay, his Bedford neighbor: "How do you do? and when will you be able to ride this far? These are my first questions. How you like the chances of the European world may be the subject of conversation but you must come with your ears stuffed full of cotton to

Jefferson's notes on the construction of the roof.
Alderman Library, University of Virginia.

fortify them against the noise of hammers, saws, planes etc. which assail us in every direction." Long before this the house had been occupied, but unfinished details, alterations, and improvements continued throughout the years, as was Jefferson's way.

Several drawings for Poplar Forest preserved in the collection of Thomas Jefferson Coolidge, Jr., are included in *Thomas Jefferson, Architect,* printed in 1916 for private distribution, with notes by Fiske Kimball. The "plan for Bedford" and "studies for a house at Poplar Forest unexecuted" are shown and the plan finally developed is discussed. It is described as a "type hitherto unused in America—a simple regular octagon, a square top-lighted room in the centre and octagonal-ended rooms around it, meeting at the central point of each side."

As it was finally completed the house at Poplar Forest has porticoes facing north and south. The main entrance is through the north portico, at the top of a broad flight of steps. Beneath the rear portico and the long room behind it, overlooking the site of the garden, is a low arcaded basement made possible by a depression in the ground. From the front the house appears to be of only one story; from the rear, two floors are seen. Stairways are placed in small square projections on the other two cardinal faces of the house. One of these led to Jefferson's private apartment and the other to a pantry which served the central dining room. The arrangement of study alcove and dressing room was like that already used at Monticello, and plans show alcove beds there, in the east and west rooms, centered to permit use from either side.

A narrow hallway, extending from the main door into the center room, divided the octagonal section behind the north portico into two smaller hexagonal rooms; the corresponding space behind the south portico is undivided. The center room, about twenty feet square and without windows, was lighted from above. Doorways "with double leaves" in the center of each of its four walls led to oblong chambers with breadth about half their length, corners cut off and a fireplace at each end. Thus, in the octagonal unit, each of four spaces around a center square formed an irregular octagon.

An architectural curiosity of the house is a flue in a corner of the square central salon, connected to a chimney perpendicular to one of the four octagonal rooms. The square space in the lower level below this same central room provided "a dark hole" for use as a storage cellar. A second "dungeon" below this one, and of the same size, was no doubt a wine cellar. The main rooms measure fourteen feet from floor to ceiling, and those below stairs are eight feet in height.

Some of the drawings marked for Bedford indicate that Jefferson may have made earlier studies on a simpler scale than those finally used, for no building corresponding to them seem to have been erected. It also appears from Jefferson's papers that as the structure progressed he instructed his workman to make changes, and so exact plans of the house as it was finished do not exist.

Of the original dependencies, the kitchen and smoke house stand intact today to the east of the house. Balancing privies placed at discreet distances to each side, like two sentry boxes, imitate the house in their octagonal form and Palladian cornices. Artificial mounds, once bright with bloom, screen them from view from the

View from the west,
showing north and south porticoes.

South portico
and basement arcade.

house. These were ornamented with shrubs, according to Jefferson's planting notes, which tell just where he placed calycanthus, lilac, althea, roses, golden willows, weeping willows, Athenian and Lombardy poplars. One notation shows that he planted "19 paper mulberries in a clump between the W. cloacina and fence" and the same "between the E. cloacina and fence." Grass plots equidistant from the eight sides of the house were enclosed by a fence shaped in eight equal angles.

In memoranda to Jeremiah A. Goodman, the overseer at Poplar Forest, are these instructions under date of December 1811: "The ground laid off for my garden is to be inclosed with a picquet fence, 7 feet high, so close that a hare cannot get into it. It is 80 yards square, will take I suppose about 2400 rails of 8 f. long besides the running rails and stakes, the sheep to be folded in it every night." The same papers indicate that plantation activities were well established at Poplar Forest by this date.

A circular drive from the public road formed the approach to the house, but the boxwood planting seen today in the center plot formed within the roadway does not date from Jefferson's time: he seems not to have cared

for boxwood. The maze usually attributed to him was created by a later owner.

In a letter to John Wayles Eppes from Monticello dated September 18, 1812 (quoted in the Huntington Library *Quarterly*, Vol. 6, No. 3), Jefferson reported progress up to that time, giving also his own estimate of the cost and quality of the house. The letter describes it as "an octagon of 50 f. diameter, of brick, well built, will be plaistered this fall, when nothing will be wanting to finish it completely but the cornices and some of the doors. When finished it will be the best dwelling house in the state, except that of Monticello, preferable to that, as more proportioned to the faculties of a private citizen. I shall probably go on with the cornices and doors at my leisure at Monticello and in planting and improving the grounds around it. I have just paid between 3 and 4000 dollars cash for the building, besides doing all the planter's work, which is fully the half, so that its cost may be very moderately rated at 6,000 D."

In a later letter to Eppes, this one dated July 16, 1814, Jefferson relates that since their "correspondence on the subject . . . much towards its completion" had gone forward at Poplar Forest. "The inside work is mostly

West cloacina and
mound screening it
from the house.

The dependencies at Poplar Forest:
kitchen and smoke house.

done and I have this summer built a wing of offices 110 feet long, in the manner of those at Monticello, with a flat roof in the level of the house. The whole, as it now stands, could not be valued at less than 10,000 D. and I am going on. I am also making such improvements of the grounds as require time to perfect themselves." This letter indicates that offices once existed there, although no trace of them is seen today and work to uncover foundation remains has not been undertaken.

Among the Jefferson papers in the Massachusetts Historical Society is a letter written from Poplar Forest on August 31, 1817, to Martha Jefferson Randolph that tells of continuing building operations even at that late date. "Ellen and Cornelia are the severest students I have ever seen. They never leave their room but to come to meals . . . An alteration in their part of the house not yet finished has deprived them of the use of their room longer than I had expected, but two or three days will now restore it to them."

In 1819 Jefferson spent two months of the summer at Poplar Forest, and while there supervised the laying of a marble hearth and the plastering of the ceiling of the dining room. The year before he had written Lafayette of his failing health: "the hand of age, my dear friend, has been pressing heavily on me for the last few years and has rendered me unequal to the punctualities of correspondence." The trips to Bedford were to continue for several years more, despite his frailties. On April 13, 1820, he wrote William Short: "I can walk the round of my garden; not more. But I ride six or eight miles a day without fatigue. I shall set out for Poplar Forest within three or four days; a journey from which my physician augurs much good." In the spring of 1823 he made his last trip there, although in the spring of the following year and again in 1825 he mentioned proposed trips that evidently did not materialize.

Jefferson bequeathed the house and a large portion of the original Poplar Forest acreage to his grandson, Francis Eppes. In 1828, two years after becoming its owner, Eppes sold it to William Cobbs, whose father was a neighbor and friend of the builder. Cobbs willed the mansion and the lands purchased with it to his daughter Emily, who had married Edward S. Hutter, a young naval officer. From them it was inherited by a son, Christian S. Hutter. Upon his death in 1946, after being in one family for 118 years, it was again sold—this time to the present owners, Mr. and Mrs. James Owen Watts, Jr., who make it their year-round home.

Main façade of The Vale, from a photograph taken before 1880. Except for the Doric front porch, an early addition, the house is seen here as McIntire designed it, before the 1882 alterations changed its appearance.

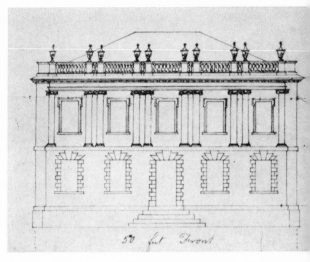

McIntire's elevation of the central portion of the Lyman house. It is doubtful if the urns were ever executed. *Courtesy Essex Institute.*

A McIntire country house

BY BERTRAM K. LITTLE

To THE EAST of the juncture of the present-day Beaver and Lyman Streets, in Waltham, Massachusetts, opposite the site of the town's first meetinghouse, is one of the most important early country seats in the United States, an outstanding combination of planning, planting, mansion, stable, and greenhouses.

It is appropriately named The Vale. Something in the sweep of meadows from a swift-running brook to a protecting rocky, wooded ridge on the north must have appealed to Theodore Lyman when, in March 1793, he purchased a tract of land here from Jonas Dix, Jr. He probably decided from the beginning to place a pleasure garden in the lee of the ridge, marking its northern boundary by a winding brick wall with peach trees trained against the warm south side; and to provide a serene retreat by surrounding a velvety lawn with fruit and ornamental trees, various shrubs, and box-bordered flower beds. This plan has remained unaltered to the present day.

At forty Theodore Lyman had formed the nucleus of his fortune, through his fur-trading ventures to the Pacific Northwest and the Far East, and had acquired a wide knowledge of the world of art and culture. He wanted to build a country seat where he could enjoy leisure and privacy and pursue the interest in farming which had led him to aid in the founding of the Massachusetts Society for the Promotion of Agriculture the year before he bought the Dix property.

He sought the advice of William Bell, an English gardener, in laying out the grounds following the naturalistic theories of Humphrey Repton and in planting the trees—English elms, oaks, pines, copper beeches—which are so impressive today. For his architect Lyman chose one from his wife's native town of Salem, whose reputa-

tion was steadily growing, Samuel McIntire. The Lyman house is the only known example of a building outside Essex County erected from McIntire's designs. His original drawings for the house are in the Essex Institute in Salem; all have his distinctive handwritten notes and one of them his signature.

It is not certain just when the mansion was completed, but construction must have been started soon after 1793. The east, or ballroom, wing was apparently built later than the rest of the house, since there was at one time a window where today the door opens into the ballroom from the east parlor. It must have been only a short time later, however, for the sectional drawing of the east wing is executed on the same paper as the other plans and bears a note to the effect that it "takes up the height of two Stories—tho. withoutside it must be finished as if there were two to make it uniform with the other wing."

Extensive alterations in 1882 changed the appearance of the house a good deal. A third story was added in the center, the west, or "kitchen," wing was enlarged and remodeled, and two-story bays were built on either side of the front door. Fortunately, however, two of the principal rooms—the famed oval parlor and the ballroom—remain today as fine untouched examples of McIntire's work; three others retain much of their early feeling because of sympathetic restoration in 1918; and the two main bedrooms, except for the rectangular bays, are much as McIntire designed them. Some of the original Ionic pilasters on the façade and the balusters on the roof were kept in the 1882 remodeling, and the architect at that time sought to preserve the balanced relationship between central mass and wings.

The subordinate buildings on the estate are of great

The pleasure garden from the east. Beyond the great copper beech can be seen the greenhouse built about 1804.

The Vale in Waltham, Massachusetts

Except as noted, photographs by George M. Cushing, Jr.

The famed oval drawing room, or bow parlor. Its original furnishings, left as a memorial to the last owners, Arthur and Susan Cabot Lyman, include two banquettes designed and executed by Samuel McIntire for the recessed windows in which they still stand. The pair of lacquered tables was secured by the first Theodore Lyman in the course of his trading ventures in the Far East. *Above,* one of the three curved doorways in the bow parlor, with characteristic McIntire ornament. The projecting end blocks of the overdoors are embellished with carved urns and the panels between with applied swags and clusters of acorns and oak leaves.

JUNE 1953

507

interest. At the northwest corner of the garden stands a long greenhouse built about 1804, with the original heating arrangement of arches and flues at the base of the heavy brick rear wall. In this and the other greenhouses one may today see camellia bushes higher than one's head and grapevines with main stems as big as one's fist. A handsome stable, unmistakably built from a McIntire design, has the central pavilion and massive archivolt and keystone typical of his earlier work. At the angle of the peach wall is a light, graceful McIntire summer house.

From generation to generation The Vale descended in the family from father to son, until it was presented to the Society for the Preservation of New England Antiquities by the five children of the late Arthur and Susan C. Lyman. To mark its opening to the public for the first time a loan exhibition of American furniture and other decorative arts of the period was held at the Lyman house during the summer of 1952. The estate will be open to the public through the summer to the middle of September, with a special loan exhibition this year featuring landscape paintings and botanical prints.

The east parlor, as it appeared during the opening loan exhibition. The Bilbao mirror (c. 1770) over the mantel is flanked by a pair of Queen Anne needlework pictures (English, c. 1720). The flower holders on the shelf are marked *Eastwood* (English, c. 1800). On the mahogany birdcage tip table (American, c. 1770) is a partial set of Chinese export porcelain. The Hepplewhite mahogany armchair is attributed to Samuel McIntire (Salem, c. 1795).

Typical arched recesses, dado, and shuttered windows are repeated in the dining room, opposite the east parlor, but with subtle differences in decorative detail. Above the fireplace, with its blue Delft landscape tiles, is a portrait by Ethan Allen Greenwood, and on the mantel stands a pair of eighteenth-century English enamel candlesticks. Beyond the Massachusetts Sheraton chairs (c. 1800) may be seen an unusual small sideboard (New England, c. 1780).

HISTORY IN HOUSES

Bartow Mansion

By JOSEPH DOWNS

For many years Curator of the American Wing at the Metropolitan Museum of Art, Mr. Downs is now Curator of the Henry F. du Pont Collection at Winterthur, Delaware. He will continue as consultant to the American Wing.

Bolton's *Guide to New Rochelle* published in 1842 takes note of a country house that still stands facing the Sound at Pelham Bay, New York. ". . . The present proprietor has lately erected a fine stone house in the Grecian style, which presents a neat front, with projecting wings . . ." The fortunate owner was Robert Bartow, a descendant of Sir John Pell, second lord of the Manor of Pelham, whose house had stood near the same site from 1675 until it was destroyed soon after the Revolution.

Bartow Mansion with its simple gray ashlar exterior, ample scale, and rich interior detail, represents the best freely creative work done in the Greek Revival style. It may have been designed by the architect Minard Lafever (*1797-1854*), who was trained as a carpenter in upstate New York and came to Manhattan in 1828. He published three books of architecture between 1829 and 1835: *The Young Builder's General Instructor,* 1829; *The Modern Builder's Guide,* 1833; and *The Beauties of Modern Architecture,* 1835. Lafever was probably the most talented American designer of his time, and his work is characterized by bold modifications of classical Greek precedent. The rooms at Bartow Mansion reflect the crisp, imaginative detail that Lefever achieved in his interiors.

Robert and Maria Lorillard Bartow and their children occupied the house described by Bolton until 1888, when it was acquired, together with adjoining lands, by the City of New York for park purposes. In 1914 the International Garden Club leased the house for its headquarters, and started the development of the gardens and rehabilitation of the house. In 1939 it was taken over by the late Mayor La

The west entrance to Bartow Mansion gives a first impression of austerity that is a lasting one, from the severe, cut stone of the facade, relieved only by a heavy white painted cornice and beveled quoins of dressed stone, and the outsweeping iron balustrade flanking the double paneled doors. The rich planting of trees, shrubs, and perennials planned so wisely and maintained so well through the past thirty-five years, does much to soften the forbidding exterior.

Guardia as a summer "White House." In 1945 the president of the Garden Club, the late Mrs. H. Edward Manville, chose a committee for the restoration of the principal rooms at Bartow Mansion for public exhibition; Miss Agnes Miles Carpenter, the chairman of the museum committee, had the counsel of the curators of the Museum of the City of New York, the Brooklyn Museum, and the Metropolitan Museum of Art. The Department of Parks generously made the necessary repairs and renovations. The City's museums and individuals lent appropriate paintings, furniture, and other decorative art, and the house was opened to the public in May 1946.

Further work to perfect the installation continued under the leadership of the next president, Mrs. Eliot Tuckerman. At this time important and permanent objects were acquired by gifts, chiefly the handsome chandeliers on the first floor, the French carpet in the parlor, and the curtains in the two large rooms. These last were the gift of Miss Carpenter, and were executed by Frank D. Cangin and Sons.

The entrance hall, with a formally balanced arrangement of "Greek" door and window architraves, painted white against Pompeian pink walls, typifies a fresh neo-classic design in American houses. The shallow niche, repeated on the east and west facades, originally held sculptures, now lost, to strengthen the classic tie, a happy scheme to achieve dignity in an unexpected way. A marble bust of a Roman emperor now stands opposite the entrance door; at the right, above a large Empire sofa, hangs a classical version of the Prodigal Son, by Benjamin West. The hall lantern and wall lights are earlier than the house, dating from the late eighteenth century.

THE PARLOR AND DINING ROOM are distinguished by spaciousness of scale, dignity of plan, and the use of symmetrically balanced elements. The pediments enriched with spread eagle and winged cupid, and pilasters carved with acanthus and honeysuckle, give a new understanding of the Greek Revival at its best. Following contemporary precedent, the walls here have been painted pale reddish brown, to offset the marble-white woodwork, mahogany doors, and black floors. The lustrous satin curtains of copper color and robin's-egg blue, with under curtains of white mull, repeat the colors in the old French carpet. On the walls are portraits by Waldo and Jewett from the 1830's. The fine chandelier and mantel lamps, with original hurricane shades, were made about 1810; the bronze table lamps are a decade or two later. The mantel clock is French, of gilded bronze, flanked by a figure of Washington. The Empire furniture is suitable in scale to its background. The paintings in all the rooms were lent by the Metropolitan Museum of Art.

ALL THE FLOWERS used in the rooms at Bartow Mansion were grown there. Through the long French windows facing east, the visitor glimpses the terraced gardens, and the water of Pelham Bay in the distance. Between the windows of the parlor hangs a portrait of Captain Henry Rice by Gilbert Stuart, above a curio cabinet of rosewood and ormolu. The piano in the foreground is also cased in rosewood, and is signed: *John Geib & Sons New York*; upon it stands a bronze and cut-glass oil lamp, fashionable in the 1830's when Bartow was newly built, which is stamped: *P. Gardiner N. York*. At the window a music stand does double duty as a table; its top may be lifted to support music for a quartet. Here the pattern in the Savonnerie carpet *(c. 1830)* shows the softening from Napoleonic rigidity to more natural forms during the Charles X period, although still held in balanced formality. This carpet was purchased for the room by Mrs. Eliot Tuckerman, Mrs. Arthur Schermerhorn, Miss Alice Maynard, and Miss Agnes M. Carpenter.

THROUGHOUT THE ROOMS the furniture is homogeneous with the woodwork in its monumental scale and bold ornament. White marble tops for tables and sideboards, and bronze appliques or gilded stenciling to imitate them, were the chief ornaments of the mahogany and rosewood furniture of the Greek Revival period. The sideboard here has only carving to offset its massive lines; perhaps it was the unusual, cylindrical wine cupboards upon either side that won an award for its maker, Moses Beach, at a fair in Massachusetts. Above it hangs a fine girandole richly carved and gilded, which was an heirloom of the Webb family in New York and is now lent for exhibition by Mrs. Sidney G. de Kay. Arranged on the marble-topped breakfast table is a brown and green decorated porcelain chocolate service, banded in gold with the Berlin factory mark of 1844. The window hangings in the two adjoining rooms are alike, only the colors being reversed, one room having more blue, the other more copper color. The designs were adapted by Joseph Downs from several plates in *The Cabinetmaker's and Upholsterer's Guide and Repository of Designs*, published in 1826 in London by George Smith.

THE GRANDEUR achieved here by the architect a century ago is evident again in this view of the dining room. For the restoration of these handsome rooms, an attempt was made to follow the homogeneity that the background reflects, by using the same colors upon the woodwork and walls in both rooms, and the same design and fabric at all five windows, giving minor contrasts by reversing the colors, as the architect did by replacing eagles with cupids on the pediments of the dining room. The chairs and tables here are mahogany, a wood that was still the favorite of cabinetmakers in the 1830's. The mantel garniture is Siena marble and bronze, and matches the marble mantel below. The chandelier is a fine example of 1810, and, like a similar one in the parlor, was the generous gift of Harry Harkness Flagler. The walls are hung with New York landscapes painted by Jasper F. Cropsey, Thomas Doughty, and Asher B. Durand.

THE CHIEF architectural interest is confined to the first-floor rooms. Above stairs, the bedrooms are finished with plain, molded trim, and severe white marble mantels. The rooms are high-ceiled and spacious, with ample walls for the high-post beds and great wardrobes essential in early nineteenth-century houses. The background here is painted lavender, from a wall color found in Ackermann's *Repository of the Arts* dated 1837, and the woodwork is white. The mahogany bed is a fine example of New York design, made about 1820, and an heirloom of the donor, Miss Justine Erving. The summer hangings of sheer white cotton complement the handwoven bedspread; amongst the tufted floral pattern is the inscription: *Catherine Woolsey 1822.* Upon the pair of night tables at the head of the bed stand matching bronze oil lamps with cut-glass shades, together with a fine muslin cap.

THE AFTERMATH of the Revolution brought a flood of emigres to New York, and among them were numerous artisans. Charles Honore Lannuier arrived from Paris in 1805 and opened a cabinet shop at 60 Broad Street, where he was active until 1819. All of Lannuier's work echoes his French training; this bed represents his latest output in the Empire style. The *couronne de lit*, original to the bed, is held up by stout mahogany braces fixed to the head and foot posts. Never before published, this bed was originally owned by Mrs. Isaac Bell *(1791-1871)* in New York, and is lent for exhibition by her great-granddaughter. Lannuier's engraved label has been carefully preserved inside the front rail; the red damask bed curtains are not original.

IN THE BEDROOMS "Turkey carpets" are used. These are examples of the Asia Minor weaves brought over in the early days for fine American houses, in contrast with the hooked rugs which were made for farmhouses and frontier cabins. Here the Fereghan, Baksis, and Bergama carpets give a rich note of color and pattern to the dark floors. The table below the large modern mirror is one of a pair, made for Commodore Samuel Woodhouse in Philadelphia shortly after the War of 1812. Upon the New England tambour desk stands a garniture of French Empire porcelain, and above it hangs an English needlework genre picture.

Photographs by Gottscho-Schleisner

Nicholas Biddle's Andalusia,
a nineteenth-century country seat today

BY JAMES BIDDLE, *Curator, American Wing, Metropolitan Museum of Art*

Thomas U. Walter's "before" sketch of Andalusia as it appeared before 1834. It is almost identical to a view done by William Birch in the early 1800's.

Walter's water-color "after" sketch shows the 1834-1836 additions of two front parlors, a giant Doric portico, library, and service wings. The cost was $12,000. The Hephaesteum in Athens probably served as the model.

FRANCES TROLLOPE in her amusing and not always flattering commentary on the *Domestic Manners of the Americans* had this to say about a stretch of scenery she encountered journeying to Philadelphia from New York:

"The Delaware river, above Philadelphia, still flows through a landscape too level for beauty, but it is rendered interesting by a succession of gentlemen's seats, which, if less elaborately finished in architecture, and garden grounds, than the lovely villas on the Thames, are still beautiful objects to gaze upon as you float rapidly past on the broad silvery stream that washes their lawns. They present a picture of wealth and enjoyment that accords well with the noble city to which they are an appendage."

Mrs. Trollope's book was published in 1832 and the country seat known as Andalusia that she saw from her river boat did not yet carry the striking white-columned façade that makes it today one of America's most famous Greek revival houses. Rather she would have seen the broad-piazzaed, late Federal house as drawn by William Birch in the early 1800's and as painted by Thomas U. Walter in a "before" sketch for his client, Nicholas Biddle. Walter's "after" sketch shows the transformations that were to be wrought from 1834 to 1836.

In 1795 John Craig of Philadelphia purchased a farmhouse and almost one hundred acres of land on the banks of the Delaware as a summer retreat for his family. His wife sketched in a garden book the additions she wished made; shortly thereafter a three-storied house with projecting bays at either end and a wide veranda to catch the river breezes rose at the crest of a lawn which sloped gently to the water's edge. In October 1811 the Craigs' daughter, Jane, married Nicholas Biddle and Andalusia acquired its most famous owner.

At the time of his marriage Nicholas

Biddle was twenty-five, recently returned from Europe where he had served the government in Paris and London and had traveled extensively. His trip to Greece in 1806 inspired a love for classic Greece which he kept for the rest of his life and which was to have a profound influence on his taste in art and architecture. For over five years a contributor to *Port Folio,* the nation's leading literary periodical, he became editor in 1812 and devoted himself to the magazine until his return to political life and the State Senate in 1814. The year 1819 saw him appointed a director of the Second Bank of the United States by his friend President Monroe, and four years later he was elected president of that rich and powerful institution in which were deposited the funds of the United States government.

While Nicholas Biddle was editor of the *Port Folio,* it published an essay "On Architecture" by George C. Tucker which urged an uncompromising imitation of Grecian architecture. It is not surprising, therefore, that as a director of the Bank of the United States he supported the choice of William Strickland's design for the bank which was based on the Parthenon.

In 1832 and 1833, Nicholas Biddle worked with the architect Thomas U. Walter on the design of the soon-to-be-built Girard College. Indeed, worked is too mild a word. Nicholas' taste for things Greek, not to mention his prominence on the national scene, forced the college's building committee to scrap Walter's first and already approved design in favor of what Biddle described as "a perfect chaste specimen of Grecian architecture," the enormous peripteral octastyle Corinthian temple that dominates the college today.

Indulging in more of the Greek ideas that had disconcerted the Girard College building committee, Nicholas Biddle soon called again upon the amiable Thomas Walter who had so sensibly acquiesced to his taste in the design for the college. In 1834 he commissioned the architect to transform his country house into a New World Doric temple. The result, both inside and out, was recorded in Antiques for April 1952.

Andalusia was not just a house. In local parlance, it was a "seat" composed of garden and farm units. To enliven the ladies' daily strolls along meandering gravel walks, Walter scattered bits of architecture through the grounds. There was a two-storied columned Billiard Room for the gentlemen's pleasure at billiards and cards. At the foot of the lawn on the very edge of the river a ruined Gothic Grotto with stained-glass windows

Except as noted, photographs by Taylor and Dull.

Nicholas Biddle, "Czar Nicholas" to his banking enemies and builder of the Greek revival Andalusia, was painted in this romantic mood in 1826 by Thomas Sully.

stirred a delicious touch of melancholy in the viewer. For those interested in horticulture and farming, there were two enormous Graperies. Tobacco grew in fields irrigated by an elaborate system of underground pipes which brought water from the river to a tower reservoir from whence it was dispensed to greenhouses and gardens. Guernsey cows, reputedly the first brought to this country, lolled contentedly in the meadows. This, then, was the setting for Nicholas Biddle's retirement from the bank in 1839. Philip Hone described it thus in his diary notation for March 30 of that year:

"He possesses a beautiful seat on the banks of the Delaware, where there is a miniature facsimile of the monster's marble den in Chestnut Street; and he raises fine grapes and gets a good price for them

Walter's own handwriting annotates this *Design for Grotto at Mr. Biddle's Country Seat*. The finished building, as seen in the long view of the lawn, lacks the tower. Neither owner nor architect saw any discrepancy in the placing of a Gothic ruin at the foot of a lawn crowned by a Grecian temple.

in the Philadelphia market, and has as good a right to enjoy *otium cum dignitate* as anybody I know."

Upon retirement Nicholas Biddle conferred again with Walter about the possibility (never realized) of enlarging the main house at Andalusia by the addition of another wing, another story, and an enormous colonnade to surround the entire house which was to take the form of

a Greek cross. He continued his literary interests by writing articles and poetry.

The peace of Andalusia was shattered in 1841 when the bank, now the Bank of the United States of Pennsylvania, failed. The crash was disastrous to many and the victims turned in rage upon the bank's former president. His own large fortune lost in a desperate attempt to save the bank, the silver service presented to him by the bank's directors upon his retirement melted down for bullion, his country seat sold at auction, bought in for Mrs. Biddle by her sons, Nicholas Biddle withdrew for the last time into the second of his great temples. His last dinner party at Andalusia is described by J. J. Smith, an architect and associate of Walters:

"When the bank failed, and he was disgraced in public estimation, his heart was broken. The flatterers who had overpraised him now pursued him with vituperation to his solitude at Andalusia . . . He had at first been overpraised and now he was overabused. Power such as he attained was a dangerous possession . . . When his disease had assumed a serious character, few persons visited the house . . . On Christmas he invited his brother, Commodore Biddle, Mr. Bernard Henry and myself to dine and pass the day which proved a stormy one. He came downstairs about noon, and we had some very pleasant chat in his fine library . . . The old family billiard table had been brought into the library from its summer quarters [the Billiard Room] to allow indoor exercise to the invalid. I played a few short games with him and the Commodore alternately . . . He was evidently weak but kept up a flow of very cheerful conversation. At dinner he carved well a pair of capons, left the table before we did, retired to his bed, from which he never again rose to go downstairs and soon breathed his last [February 27, 1844] a victim of General Jackson's hostility to the bank, and feeling keenly the utter reverse of public opinion." (*Recollection of J. J. Smith*, 1892.)

Mrs. Biddle died a few years later, her mind tormented by memories of the past. Its creative spirit gone, Andalusia slipped unmolested through the Victorian era, a shuttered house, open in summer to provide cramped and uncomfortable quarters for the heirs, their offspring, and innumerable visiting cousins.

To accommodate the growing families a house in the Gothic taste was built on the grounds in the 1840's. The architect is not known but the house closely resembles Plate L in *Cottage and Villa Architecture*, published in Philadelphia by Thomas U. Walter and J. J. Smith in 1846. The cottage was enlarged at various times during the nineteenth century but change and improvements were shunned for Andalusia itself. The great house and its grounds passed safely into the twentieth century, to be refurbished, rather than restored, by descendants of its illustrious creator.

The neoclassic Billiard Room, at the opposite side of the lawn from the Gothic Grotto. *Photograph by Cortlandt V. D. Hubbard.*

Andalusia, Nicholas Biddle's country seat, looks today much as it did upon its completion in 1836. The portico is of wood; the columns have brick cores. The walls are stuccoed and lined to imitate dressed stone. Originally the porch floor was painted in black and white squares in imitation of marble paving.

Adhering to the classical tradition in ground plan, the Cottage is frosted with Gothic details of pointed gables, diamond-pane windows square-headed with label moldings, and boldly crenelated bays. It was originally only one bay deep, with a wooden piazza and open-work lattice columns.

An American oak bench and two side chairs in the Gothic taste in the hall of the Cottage are original to the house. The mahogany and brass jardinieres (on modern bases), hall lantern, and parlor organ are English.

Cornice and door moldings of the Cottage's double parlors reflect the classical revival that ran concurrently with the Gothic. The diamond-pane windows and the room's furnishings provide the Gothic touches. Two nearly matching English needlework carpets, done in brilliant blues, yellows, and reds, date probably 1825-1840. The *torchère*, one of a pair, is grained to imitate maple, the wood of the tall-backed Gothic chair in the foreground. These American pieces are original to Andalusia, as is the great Gothic revival bed given to Nicholas Biddle by Joseph Bonaparte about 1833, shown in ANTIQUES for May 1962 (frontispiece). Library steps in the form of a low bench, a nest of tables, and the Pugin-style armchairs in the second parlor are of English origin.

The Hermitage, home of Andrew Jackson

BY STANLEY F. HORN, *President, board of trustees, Ladies' Hermitage Association*

THE FIRST FEW years of Andrew Jackson's married life were spent on the plantations Poplar Grove and Hunter's Hill. From all accounts Hunter's Hill was a notable house for its time and place, but in 1804 a period of personal financial stringency made it necessary for Jackson to sell it. It was then that he and his wife, Rachel, took up residence on a nearby tract of four hundred and twenty acres, the nucleus of the much larger Hermitage plantation which was to be his home for the rest of his life (see ANTIQUES, September 1932, p. 96).

At the time of his removal to the Hermitage tract, Jackson could not afford to build as fine a house as the one he had left, but he and his wife adapted themselves to the rather primitive living quarters they found there.

Fig. 1. The Hermitage, built in 1819 near Nashville, was the home of Andrew Jackson (1767-1845). The two-story portico and two lateral wings were added in 1832. The house appears today as it was restored after an 1834 fire. The tall red cedars and the two stately holly trees were planted by Jackson and his friend and "artist in residence," Ralph E. W. Earl (see p. 390), when Jackson returned home from Washington in the summer of 1837, after his eight years in the White House. *Photograph by Wiles-Hood, by courtesy of the Ladies' Hermitage Association.*

By 1819, however, Jackson had the time and the means to build a more elegant residence. Rachel selected the site for the new house, the design of which was severely simple: four rooms on the ground floor, two on either side of a wide central hall, with a similar arrangement upstairs. It was here that Mrs. Jackson died in December 1828, soon after Jackson's election to the Presidency but before his inauguration.

The Jacksons had no children of their own, but in 1809 they had adopted one of the newborn twins of Mrs. Jackson's brother Severn Donelson and named him Andrew Jackson Jr. In 1831 this young man married Sarah York of Philadelphia and, acting on President Jackson's instructions, brought her to the White House for a honeymoon of several months before taking up permanent residence at the Hermitage in the spring of 1832. Jackson, in anticipation of this expansion of his household, had arranged for some additions to the house, including a two-story portico at the front entrance and a one-story wing at each end of the building.

Jackson had also arranged to have the house stocked with provisions and some additional furniture, and he wrote to Andrew suggesting that Sarah let him know if she

Fig. 2. The sideboard and dining table were bought for the dining room by Jackson and his wife from François Seignouret in New Orleans in May 1821. (Seignouret, then a prominent cabinetmaker, in 1815 had served as a member of the *Bataillon d'Orléans* under Jackson in the battle of New Orleans.) Over the sideboard are portraits by Ralph E. W. Earl of Jackson's adopted son, Andrew Jackson Jr., and his wife, Sarah; the portraits at the right are of General Jackson and his wife, Rachel. The candelabra and epergne on the table, as well as the other silver seen here, were also part of the original furnishings. Traditionally, the six klismos-type chairs at the table were presented to Jackson by John Overton, his former law partner and lifelong friend and adviser; they are identical with six chairs now to be seen in the dining room at Travellers' Rest (p. 400), Overton's home near Nashville, and it is an established fact that Overton purchased twelve chairs of this type in Philadelphia in 1824. The marble-topped pier table at the right is believed to be one of the pair purchased by Jackson from Barry and Krickbaum in Philadelphia in February 1837; its mate is in the front parlor

Except as noted, photographs are by Helga Photo Studio.

wanted anything further to facilitate her housekeeping. Sarah was not slow to accept the invitation, and within a few days wrote her distinguished father-in-law that a new carpet was needed for the dining room, as well as linen and some additional silverware for the table—all of which were promptly supplied through Henry Toland, a Philadelphia merchant and friend of Jackson.

The young Jacksons were to have less than three years to enjoy their new home, for in October 1834 the house was so severely damaged by fire that all except the standing walls had to be rebuilt. Jackson, in the White House, accepted the calamity with resignation and equanimity and wrote to Andrew: "Tell Sarah to cease to mourn its loss. I will have it rebuilt . . . Give me as accurate an account of the loss of furniture as you can at as early a period as possible." Fortunately the furniture and other contents of the downstairs rooms, including Jackson's books and papers, were saved, but all the bedroom furniture upstairs was destroyed and had to be replaced.

Immediately after the Hermitage burned, Jackson instructed his son to "Let workmen be employed forthwith to repair it," but he did not depend entirely on Andrew to get it done. He wrote also to his trusted friend Colonel Robert Armstrong, who called into consultation another

of Jackson's friends, Colonel Charles J. Love. In January Colonel Love wrote to the President that "a contract has been made with Messrs. Rife and Hume for the rebuilding of the house at the Hermitage . . . The materials are to be good and the work executed in the best possible style. Mr. Hume is now up the country to make engagements for the lumber that it may be got down in time to have it well seasoned before the work is put together."

The "Rife and Hume" referred to in Colonel Love's letter were Joseph Reiff and William C. Hume, the carpenter-contractors who were then employed in constructing the handsome house which General Jackson was having built on the Tulip Grove plantation nearby for his wife's nephew, Andrew Jackson Donelson. Although not trained architects, Reiff and Hume had books of basic designs of such neoclassical architectural features as circular staircases and Palladian windows. Their contract with Jackson was dated January 1, 1835, and provided for completion of the Hermitage by December 25, 1835; but it was not actually finished and ready for occupancy until the following summer. Its exterior appearance then was the same as it is now, as there have been no additions or other structural alterations.

When Jackson died in 1845 he left the entire Hermitage estate of twelve hundred acres to his adopted son. Before he died he instructed Andrew that if ever it became necessary for him to sell the property he should give the State of Tennessee the first opportunity to buy it. This necessity arose in 1856, by which time Andrew had already sold off seven hundred acres. He accordingly offered to sell the house and the remaining five hundred acres to the state, and the general assembly enacted legislation authorizing the governor to purchase the property. It was agreed that the Jackson family could rent and occupy the place for two years.

The legislation also provided that the governor was "authorized and required" to tender the property to the government of the United States, "to be used as a site for a branch of the Military Academy at West Point," further providing that if the Federal government did not accept the offer within two years, "then the governor shall be authorized and required to have fifty acres laid off, including the tomb, mansion and the spring and the spring houses, and expose the balance to public sale either as a whole or in lots . . . and make his report to the legislature of 1859-1860."

Andrew Johnson was governor of Tennessee at the time, and he was a sponsor of the plan to offer the Hermitage estate as a site for a Southern branch of the national military academy. He lost no time in making the required tender, and in 1857 the Senate's committee on military affairs accepted it. But the war clouds were gathering; there was mounting sentiment in the North against a Federal military academy anywhere in the South —and so the state retained title to the Hermitage property, without any very definite idea as to what should be done with it.

The Jackson family, when the two years of prepaid rent expired in 1858, moved to Mississippi. For the next

Fig. 3. Jackson's library still contains his bookcase, tables, and chairs. The swivel chair at the secretary was made of wood from the frigate *Constitution* (*Old Ironsides*) and used by Levi Woodbury, Secretary of the Navy in Jackson's cabinet. In the corner is a marble bust of Jackson done by Hiram Powers before the sculptor went to Italy to study in 1837. On the candlestand in the foreground are displayed Jackson's Bible, spectacles, and brass candlestick.

two years the house remained vacant and the fields untilled, both suffering the natural effects of neglect. Then in 1860 Isham G. Harris was elected governor of Tennessee, and one of his first acts was to invite Jackson to return with his family to the Hermitage and serve as its custodian, living there as a tenant at will. So the family returned to their old home: Andrew Jackson Jr. and his wife, Sarah; their daughter, Rachel; and their two sons, Andrew and Samuel—together with Sarah's widowed sister, Marion Adams, and her three sons. Nothing more was said about establishing a military school there or selling the property off in building lots. Indeed, what to do with the Hermitage was one of the state government's least pressing problems in 1860 and 1861 as Tennessee was rapidly moving toward casting its lot with the new Confederate States of America.

In 1861 the Jacksons' two sons and the three sons of Mrs. Adams joined the Confederate armed forces. Of the five only Colonel Andrew Jackson III lived to return to the Hermitage. In 1862 Nashville was captured by the Federal troops, and during the remaining years of the war the Hermitage was protected by a troop of Federal cavalry, placed there by General George H. Thomas; because of his foresight the Hermitage escaped damage during the war years. In April 1865, just as the war was ending, Andrew Jackson Jr. died from an accidental wound suffered while hunting. His daughter had married and moved to a nearby farm, so his widow and Mrs. Adams were left the only occupants of the house until Colonel Jackson returned home late in the summer of 1865.

Sarah Jackson, her son, and her sister remained at the Hermitage as custodians and guests of the state. In 1887 Mrs. Jackson died and was succeeded as custodian by her son, who, in the same year, married Amy Rich, a native of Ohio teaching school in the neighborhood. As the postwar years rolled by, various suggestions were made about the use of the Hermitage property; but during the two decades following 1865 most of the efforts of the people of Tennessee were devoted to recuperation from the ravages of the war and no serious consideration was given any plan for the Hermitage.

In 1889, when the increasingly shabby house was being considered as a residence for veterans of the Confederate army, the Ladies' Hermitage Association was organized for the purpose of saving Old Hickory's home from misuse or destruction. A compromise was reached: the state would retain four hundred and seventy-five acres of the farm and on it put up a building for the soldiers' home, granting to the women's organization control of the Hermitage itself and twenty-five acres immediately adjoining it, including the garden and tomb. Later, when the need for a soldier's home had ended, that section of the property was added to the part originally granted the association, restoring the acreage to what it was when the state acquired it in 1856.

Due to the fortunate circumstance that the Hermitage was occupied exclusively by the Jackson family until it was turned over to the association, the furniture and furnishings to be seen there today are original pieces bought and used by Andrew Jackson during his lifetime and, later, by Andrew Jackson Jr. and his family.

Fig. 4. Jackson's bedroom appears today as it was the day he died. The bed is probably one of the "6 Mahogany bedsteads" bought from George W. South, of Philadelphia, in January 1838, along with the "4 Curtins, Crimson Silk lined with white Silk and full mounted" and other furnishings purchased to replace those burned in the 1834 fire. The "curtins" on the bed and at the windows are exact duplicates of the originals, which are now in storage for preservation. The cotton bedspread with Jackson's wife's initials *R. J.* embroidered on it, is also a reproduction of the original, which is displayed in the museum nearby. The portrait, painted by Ralph E. W. Earl, is of little Rachel, daughter of Jackson's adopted son.

Fig. 5. Since the furniture on the lower floor was not destroyed in the 1834 fire, this mahogany bedstead in the ground-floor bedroom across the hall from Jackson's own may be one of those purchased from Seignouret in New Orleans in 1821—or it may be one of six bedsteads bought in 1838 from South to furnish the rebuilt Hermitage. That purchase included "2 large size bureaus" apparently bought for this room and Jackson's bedroom (Fig. 4). It seems likely that the marble-topped washstand at the left here and its mate in the room across the hall were also bought from South. The same is true of the round marble-topped table in the foreground, the mate of which may be seen in Fig. 6. The portrait of Mrs. Andrew Jackson Jr. was painted by G. P. A. Healy when (commissioned by Louis Philippe) he visited the Hermitage in 1845 to paint Jackson's portrait to hang in Paris beside one of Washington.

For other illustrations, see color insert.

Fig. 6. Most of the furniture in this southwest bedroom on the second floor was included in the lot purchased in 1837 from the Philadelphia firm of Barry and Krickbaum: "1 large wardrobe . . . 1 elliptic front bureau . . . 1 work table, elegantly fitted up." The bedstead is probably one of those bought in 1836 from South. In the foreground is an upholstered chair, once in Lafayette's château in France, which was presented to the Ladies' Hermitage Association in 1890 by the marquis' grandson Senator Edmond de Lafayette.

Preserving the not-so-old

BY BARBARA SNOW

THE SAME PAINSTAKING RESEARCH that has been responsible for the successful restoration of seventeenth- and eighteenth-century houses is now being applied to the last century and has brought a new appreciation of a period that is much less remote. The restoration of Fountain Elms, preserving as it does much of the atmosphere of Victorian America and reflecting a taste that is today regarded with affectionate amusement, emphasizes the wisdom of salvaging examples of this chapter in the country's architectural development while contemporary records and, in some cases, memories, are readily available for reference. We have selected a few other historic mid-nineteenth-century houses from various sections of the country brought to our attention by the National Trust for Historic Preservation, which has long championed the cause of the nineteenth century and has done more than any other single agent to help local groups in their struggle to preserve historic buildings of every period.

This dramatic night view of Sturdivant Hall, Selma, Alabama, captures all of the romance associated with the neoclassic plantation houses of the South. Built in 1853 for Edward T. Watts, the mansion changed hands twice during the 1864-1870 period. In 1870 it was bought by the Gillman family, who sold it to the city in 1957. Restored and refurnished by grants from the Sturdivant Museum Association and city and county governing bodies, it now houses the collections of Robert D. Sturdivant and his wife. (Mr. Sturdivant provided funds for the museum in his will.) The mansion is a great square of stuccoed brick with a sixty-foot veranda across the front; six fluted Corinthian columns support the veranda roof and two smaller columns within the pilasters flank the front door. The door opens on a marble-floored hall with double parlors on the right and another parlor and dining room on the left. Frescoed panels, carved cornices, and mantels add to the richness of the interior. Marble, iron, and plaster are intricately used to decorate both interior and exterior. This graceful example of ante-bellum architecture, now open to the public, will be used for meetings of civic groups, for receptions, and as a museum.

In neighboring Mississippi another ante-bellum house has been recently restored by its owners and will be open to the public. McRaven, in Vicksburg, traces the architectural history of that thriving river town during the first half of the nineteenth century. The earliest part of the house was built about 1797 in the typical frontier style of the region. In 1836 the middle section with Creole-inspired gallery was added (the brackets appear to have been added still later). The final section, built in 1849, incorporated the marble fireplaces, plasterwork ceilings and molding, carved window facings, and full-length windows typical of the Greek Revival. The owners, Mr. and Mrs. O. E. Bradway, restored the house and furnished it with antiques many of which are original to the house. They are active members of the Mississippi Historic Foundation which is hard at work in Vicksburg preparing historic zoning legislation to protect the city's old buildings and sites. The foundation has saved the Vick-Marshall house from destruction and is currently trying to raise funds to buy the mansion. The example set by individual members like the Bradways in the restoration and care of their own houses has been a great help to the foundation in its city-wide program.

At the time Fountain Elms and Sturdivant Hall were being built and furnished in the East and South, settlers were pushing beyond the Rockies to the Pacific coast in increasing numbers. A recently restored house in Salt Lake City, Utah, is a memorial to the Mormon pioneers who were among the first to settle beyond the Rocky Mountains, and to their leader, Brigham Young, one of the country's greatest colonizers. Beehive House was built and furnished in 1854-1855. Architecturally it has elements of the Federal style of Young's native New England as well as of the later Greek Revival of the Midwest and the South. The cupola on the house has a finial in the form of a beehive, and this symbol of Mormon industry which gives the house its name appears as a decorative motif throughout the interior. Brigham Young lived here until his death in 1877. Until 1918 it served as the official residence of succeeding presidents of the church and down to 1958 it was used for other church activities. Restoration and refurnishing were begun in 1959 and have just been completed. Like most houses of the period it had undergone extensive "improvements" in the latter part of the century, and the work of restoring it as it was during Brigham Young's life there had to be based on painstaking research through architectural evidence of original colors and materials, and through family documents. Many of the original pieces have been found and returned to the house to furnish the sixteen rooms that have been restored to their 1854-1877 appearance. There are three periods represented in the furnishings: the earliest furniture was brought west by Brigham Young (who was himself a cabinetmaker), other pieces were made for the house during his years there, and the more ornate furniture of the late Victorian era was introduced when his son John W. Young added a large rear wing. Today the house looks much as it did when it welcomed famous visitors from all over the world.

Tuscan villas, Greek temples, and Gothic churches inspired the mid-century builders. Libraries and monthly magazines offered advice on ornamental cottages, rural villas, Tudor, Gothic, and Elizabethan decor. The decade between 1850 and 1860 saw the fad for octagon houses spread across the country. The design possibilities of the eight-sided building had appealed to Jefferson, Thornton, and Latrobe early in the nineteenth century and had been used by all three. The real impetus for the octagon craze of the 1850's was a book by phrenologist Orson Fowler entitled *A Home For All*, published in 1849 and again in 1854. Fowler argued that beauty and utility should be as closely united in architecture as they are in nature and that since the octagon form was both more beautiful and "more consonant with the predominant or governing form of Nature . . . it deserves consideration." Others who gave it consideration were Samuel Sloan of Philadelphia, who designed Longwood in Natchez for Colonel Nutt; John Bullock, author of *The American Cottage Builder*, 1854; Zephaniah Baker in *The Cottage Builders' Manual*, 1856; and Charles Dwyer in *The Economic Cottage Builder*, 1856. Most of the octagon houses were simple, without the carvings, ornamental plaster, and molded cornices so popular with designers

of the period. The William G. McElroy house in San Francisco is a charming example of this type. It was built in 1861 and was one of five octagonal houses built in the city. Slated for demolition, it was bought and moved to its present site in 1952 by the National Society of the Colonial Dames of America Resident in the State of California, and was restored as a museum and headquarters of the society. It is furnished with antiques of an earlier period, carefully chosen examples of the decorative arts of the colonial and early Federal eras.

The National Society of the Colonial Dames of America in the State of Colorado is restoring the McAllister house in Colorado Springs—a charming example of the "small cottage . . . plain and simple in construction" illustrated with designs and floor plans in such books as *Hobbs's Architecture; Villas, Cottages and other Edifices* by Isaac H. Hobbs and Son, Philadelphia, 1873. It was built in 1873 by Major Henry McAllister of Philadelphia, who had come west the year before as representative of a corporation organized to develop lands along the Rio Grande and Denver Railway. The architect was George Summers, who had been brought from Philadelphia by the Colorado Springs Company to help the newly arrived settlers build well-constructed houses. Brick for the "Little House" was brought from the East, as were interior fixtures. It is to be restored to its early appearance, and some of the original furniture will be returned by Major McAllister's daughters. The building is one of the earliest in Colorado Springs—an example of the simple houses built in the fast-growing frontier communities throughout the West in the quarter-century after Fountain

Elms was completed. It is a historic landmark for local residents (some of whom remember the builder) and for visitors from the East who will gain a new appreciation of the tastes of the period when the mountain West was settled.

The parlor of the Peyton Randolph House is a large, well-proportioned room with windows on both sides, and its boldly paneled walls enclose the finest furnishings in the house. At one end stands an imposing English carved mahogany bookcase, c. 1765; some of the volumes on its shelves correspond to titles Randolph owned. A George I mahogany gaming table is set up with ivory checkers, dice cups, and dice, and English brass candlesticks. The Philadelphia Chippendale side chairs are from a set of six with a history of ownership in the Drinker family; the Pennsylvania Chippendale armchair has been owned in Tidewater Virginia since the eighteenth century. An English rococo gilded looking glass hangs above an English mahogany *torchère,* each one of a pair in the room, and the rococo mode appears again in the mahogany settee, made in England in the French taste. The colorful carpet is turkeywork, its design copied from a seventeenth-century example.

Peyton Randolph's inventory lists two tea sets with tea tables and other furniture, indicating that they were displayed in rooms rather than stored with the other ceramics. Here a remarkably complete tea service of Worcester soft-paste porcelain with *chinoiserie* decoration, c. 1760, is set out on an English mahogany tea table, with silver kettle and bowl on a stand close by. Two Philadelphia chairs from the set of six are drawn up to the table and the inviting group is presided over by an easy chair covered in English needlework of c. 1700.

Carved and gilded brackets hang on either side of the fireplace, each garnished with pieces of opaque white glass and Chelsea and China Trade porcelain. *Colonial Williamsburg photograph.*

The large bed chamber in the Peyton Randolph House is enlivened by colorful textiles, embroidered and woven, especially the dressing-table cover, the crewel hangings on the great Rhode Island mahogany bed of c. 1760, and the upholstery on the George I walnut easy chair. The stool by the dressing table and the dressing glass are English. On the Massachusetts tea table is a Chelsea porcelain tea service of the raised- and red-anchor periods, decorated with fable designs; Mrs. Randolph's will of 1780 mentions "the set of Chelsea Tea China." The tea kettle is of Canton enamel, c. 1760. *Colonial Williamsburg photograph.*

Quiet elegance is the keynote of the drawing room, highlighted by the crimson-upholstered easy chair. The Queen Anne armchair drawn up to the fireplace and the tea table are of the finest Philadelphia craftsmanship. The tea set is of English creamware, the five-piece garniture on the mantel shelf of famille rose Chinese Export porcelain. Set within the beautifully carved overmantel, still in its original state, is an English landscape of the school of Richard Wilson; fire tongs, shovel and the brass jamb hooks that hold them were found in the house during restoration. *Courtesy The Naomi Wood Collection.*

The Nathaniel Russell House

The oval music room is exceptionally imposing. Three long windows open on the wrought-iron balcony which surrounds this floor, connecting all the rooms. On the inner wall here the garden windows are reflected in a pair of tall windows with mirrored panes. Through the door is a view of the great staircase window and of the circular staircase which rises without visible support from the first to the third floor. The harp at the right was made in 1803 by Sébastien Erard. Through the harp is seen one of a pair of lyre-back chairs, probably from Baltimore. An American Empire couch, c. 1810, stands at one corner of the Karabagh rug, c. 1800. The painting of cupids over the mantel is of the school of Fragonard. On the mantel are a pair of Chelsea candelabra flanking a Regency bronze and ormolu clock. The tea service is Chamberlain Worcester, c. 1800. *Courtesy Historic Charleston Foundation.*

The great ballroom on the second floor was added c. 1800 when the Adam style was becoming popular in Charleston. The soft grays and golds of textiles and paint and the graceful plaster ornamentations of the cove ceiling combine to make this one of the loveliest rooms in the city. Among its glories are the large Aubusson carpet, the Italian chandelier with its fountain spray of pendants, the harp made by Sébastien Erard (1752-1831) during his stay in London from 1796 to 1806, a Venetian harpsichord, Georgian gilded mirrors, and family portraits. The portrait above the harpsichord, by Rembrandt Peale (1778-1860), is of Hugh Swinton Legaré, an ancestor of Mrs. J. A. Farrow, who was attorney general of the United States in 1840. Over the sofa is a portrait by Thomas Sully (1783-1872) of Mrs. Farrow's great-grandmother. *Courtesy Historic Charleston Foundation.*

Over the marble mantel in the first-floor drawing room hangs a portrait of the Reverend Francis Le Jau by John Beaufain Irving Jr. (1825-1877). On the north wall is a fine portrait by Jeremiah Theus (c. 1719-1774) of Mrs. Jacob Motte Sr., mother-in-law of Rebecca Motte who lived in the Brewton House during the Revolution. (She was a sister of the builder and inherited the house when her brother and his wife and children were lost at sea.) The New York table under the painting was made by Charles-Honoré Lannuier (1779-1819). The two armchairs on either side of it were made by Thomas Elfe of Charleston (c. 1719-1775) and are part of the original set of twelve, of which eight are now in the house. In the center of the room is a Queen Anne card table made in Charleston c. 1760. Pieces of China Trade porcelain bought by Miles Brewton for his new home stand on both tables. The chandelier was brought from a family plantation at Waccamaw Neck in 1791. *Courtesy Historic Charleston Foundation.*

The Miles Brewton House

The stair hall of the Hermitage, home of Andrew Jackson, is papered with scenes from the story of Telemachus printed by Dufour in Paris c. 1825 and purchased by Jackson in 1836. The matching sofas on either side of the hall were in the house when it was bought in 1856 by the state from the Jackson family.

The front parlor of the Hermitage contains furniture Jackson
bought for the home in New Orleans and Philadelphia between
1821 and 1837, including the marble-topped pier table that
matches one in the dining room and the mirror over the mantel.
The rococo revival furniture was probably bought by Jackson's
daughter-in-law in Philadelphia after his death.

In the parlor the mirror and French gilt-bronze chandelier are both from the Taggart house built in 1850 in Watertown, New York, and the white marble mantel of similar date is from a nearby house in Utica. Chairs, center table, sofa, and *étagère* were made by John Belter, of New York City (w. 1844-1863), in the late 1840's for a Syracuse client. The Williamses purchased the labeled side table at left, one of a pair, from C. A. Baudoline of New York City; the table at right was the work of Elijah Galusha of Troy (1804-1871). The garniture of porcelain mounted in gilt bronze is French and came from Johnstown, New York. The gilt cornice is from Palatine Bridge, New York; also of New York origin is the cornice in the dining room. The painting over the sofa, by Joshua Shaw (c. 1777-1860), is entitled *Early Morning, A Dream of Carthage: Dido and Aeneas Departing for the Hunt*. On the center table is an English astral lamp, with the mark of Smethurs of 138 New Bond Street, London. The papier-mâché tilt-top table in front of the window is also an English piece. *Munson-Williams-Proctor Institute.*

The Winedale Stagecoach Inn near Round Top, Texas

BY ANNA BRIGHTMAN, *Professor, University of Texas*

TRAVELERS ON THE stage route from Bastrop to San Felipe, Texas, in the 1850's and 1860's, must have found the halt at "Sam Lewis' Stopping Place" a welcome relief from the rough trip over corduroy roads. Located in the rolling meadowland between the Brazos and Colorado Rivers, the building known today as the Winedale Stagecoach Inn (Fig. 1) stands in the heart of a fertile area settled during the Mexican colonial period. The inn has been restored and finished by Miss Ima Hogg of Houston to present the appearance it had when it served as a rest stop in Texas pioneer days.

In 1848 Samuel K. Lewis, a congressman of the short-lived Republic of Texas, purchased the place and more than doubled the size of the original dwelling to make it suitable for the inn which he operated from 1849 until after the Civil War (Fig. 2). Though the village of Winedale did not yet exist, many colonists and traders traveled this way in Lewis' time. Two early routes, the Gotier Trace and the Upper La Bahia Road, which gave access to the western frontier and to Mexico, intersected nearby. At one time the United States mail stage followed a trail past the old inn.

The Winedale Inn originally was a small pioneer homestead. The oldest part, the south half, was erected by William S. Townsend, a settler from South Carolina who received his land grant from the Mexican government in 1831. After his marriage to Mary Burnam in 1834, he built a stout frame house consisting of one large room, with a fireplace, and a loft above. The shed rooms at the back, upstairs and down, were probably added as his family increased.

At some later date, the loft was turned into a full second story and an identical section was added to the north with an open passageway, or "dogtrot," between the two halves on both levels. A wide two-story gallery was also built across the front. All indications are that Sam Lewis made these later additions, since he would have needed a larger structure to serve as an inn.

After Lewis' death in 1867, his family held the property until 1882 when it was sold to Joseph George Wagner, a German immigrant. (Wagner's son, Joseph Jr., lived here until 1960.) During these years a kitchen was built on at the rear, replacing the original separate kitchen building, and the dogtrot was enclosed. These later additions have been removed in order to restore the building to its mid-nineteenth-century form.

In structure and detail the inn combines English and German features. The architectural form of the building

Fig. 1. The Winedale Stagecoach Inn is a striking landmark with its pale yellow walls and dark brown trim. The painting of the cedar pillars was determined from traces on the original posts and from the old photograph reproduced here (Fig. 2). The design on the lower sections is a *trompe l'oeil* device for suggesting the chamfered posts found on several German-built houses in the area. The large chimneys are of native stone.

is English, while the stylistic detail and craftsmanship are German. This fusion of elements typifies the blending of divergent cultures in many early Texas settlements. Simplicity characterizes the layout of the eight rooms, with two rooms on each side of the passageway on both the first and second floors. The front rooms, each with a fireplace, are considerably larger than those at the rear. The frame, siding, floors, and shake (shingle) roof are all of cedar cut on the place. The timbers are put together in the medieval carpentry style of mortised, notched, and pegged joints. The fine workmanship visible in door and window frames attests the skill of the early German craftsman.

An outstanding feature of the inn is the decorative painting of the ceiling and border in the main upstairs parlor (Figs. 3, 4). The freehand painting is surprisingly sophisticated in color and detail. Although reminiscent of the neoclassic garlands, rinceaux, and arabesques of Robert Adam, the designs have a distinct German flavor in the treatment of native floral and fruit forms. The work is attributed to Rudolph Melchior, a German artist who came to Texas in 1853 and settled in the nearby village of Round Top. Melchior's *Tage Buch* for 1853 contains several scraps of paper with designs that are related in style and detail to the work at Winedale. A similar painted ceiling in a nearby house has been documented as the work of Melchior. Two other rooms in the inn have decorative borders, one a less skilled rendition of floral garlands and the other a crude stenciled design.

Unusual colors and their unexpected combinations lend distinction and charm to the simple horizontal plank walls of all the interiors. The room with decorated ceiling has a plum-color dado topped with a narrow band of peacock blue, green walls, and paler Adam green and white as background colors for the borders and ceiling. The use of off-shades of blue and green or an extraordinary color combination such as the red-brown, salmon pink, and blue-gray in another room of the inn is characteristic of several nineteenth-century interiors in houses

nearby. The rooms of the inn are further enriched with doors painted in an exaggerated wood grain in brown over a deep yellow background. The fireplace mantels are either plain, false grained, or painted with a spatter of colors mixed with sand in imitation of stone.

No records exist to tell how the inn was furnished in Lewis' time. Where possible, Texas pieces in the provincial Biedermeier style typical of the nineteenth-century work of German craftsmen in the region have been chosen to furnish the rooms. Simple slat-back chairs with cowhide seats, cupboards, tables, and a four-poster bed of Texas origin are also displayed. The rest of the furniture is representative of German cabinetmaking in other sections of the country.

As the restoration progressed, Miss Hogg envisioned Winedale as an appropriate setting for studies and research relating to the history and the cultural contributions of the ethnic groups, primarily German, that settled central Texas. In June 1965 she gave the property, with an endowment for its support, to the University of Texas to be used in connection with programs in Texas architectural history, arts and letters, and Texas-German intellectual and social history. Miss Hogg continued her supervision in conjunction with the university's restoration architect and architectural historian. The two old barns were restored, two early log buildings were brought in and placed where the separate kitchen and smokehouse probably stood in Lewis' day, and two nineteenth-century Texas houses were moved to the site. In addition to the inn, which was opened to the public as a museum in April 1967, the larger barn has been equipped to serve as a small theater. The 1850 pioneer dwelling, Hazel's Lone Oak Cottage, serves as office and special exhibition area. The Lauderdale House, an example of Texas classic revival, provides for seminar and conference groups, and has dormitory space and a modern kitchen. Today, Winedale offers a rich environment for closer study and deeper understanding of the cultural forces which helped to shape Texas.

Fig. 2. The Winedale Inn as it looked c. 1890 when it was the home of the family of Joseph George Wagner. The dividing line of the roof between the early structure and Lewis' addition on the right can be seen clearly. *University of Texas Architectural Archives.*

Fig. 3. The upstairs parlor was probably used by the family and distinguished travelers. Its ceiling (Fig. 4), border, and overmantel decoration are the freehand work of a skilled painter, Rudolph Melchior. The fine ornamental trim contrasts markedly with the simple construction of the board ceiling and walls and the cedar plank floors used throughout the inn. The center table, made nearby in the Texas Biedermeier style, belonged to the first Wagner who settled in the area in 1853. The day bed, too, is characteristic of Texas German work in the Empire or Biedermeier style. The painted rocking chair, bridal box, and side chair are Pennsylvania German pieces.

Fig. 4. The decoration of the ceiling in the upstairs parlor, painted before the Civil War, is remarkably well preserved. In each of the classical arabesques which divide the rectangular ceiling into quarters is a symbol of one of the four seasons. A central wreath of morning-glory vines frames a green parrot, a favorite German motif.

Fig. 5. In the lower north front room the paint at the top of the walls was removed to reveal the painted floral border underneath. (This room and the little one behind it are the only ones which appear to have been painted over.) The overmantel decoration consists of a green vase with coral roses and scrolling vines with trumpet flowers against a white background. The nineteenth-century Texas-made table has the curved legs characteristic of the Texas Biedermeier style. The painted chairs are Pennsylvania German of the same era.

Fig. 6. The focal point in the Texas bedroom is the low-post bed made in nearby Independence. The bed is evidently of mesquite wood, plentiful in Texas but rarely used for furniture. The scrolled headboard and the shape of the heavy posts recall other country Empire forms. Rope lacings hold the corn-shuck "spring" and feather bed covered with an early patchwork quilt. The Texas chest of drawers in the Empire style is made of yellow pine from the Lost Pine Forest near Bastrop.

Fig. 7. Slat-back chairs with cowhide seats were common in Texas in the nineteenth century. The flattened posts and the narrowing of the leg to form a foot are Midwestern features. Considerable variation in the size and shaping of the slats can be noted among the several hide-bottom chairs used throughout the inn.

Fig. 8. Two nineteenth-century cupboards showing Biedermeier influence, this one from a German settlement in Wisconsin and the one from Texas in Fig. 9, have remarkably similar moldings and curved corners at the top. The Wisconsin cupboard is of cherry and poplar with painted graining in the center panels of the lower doors. The blue paint of the interior is a pleasing background for the display of gaudy Dutch in the strawberry pattern.

Fig. 9. This cupboard, made in Round Top, Texas, by a German cabinetmaker named Etzel, is of native cedar with warm brown painted graining. Although the Wisconsin piece in Fig. 8 has more elaborate detail in the narrow pediment, molded center drawers, and curved apron, the Texas piece reveals excellent craftsmanship in the well-fitted pegged joints, paneled sides, and molded base. A few plates in the *Texian Campaigne* pattern, c. 1848, are displayed, on the top shelf, with other commemorative china.

Exterior view. This façade of the house, with all six of the flags that have flown over Texas unfurled above the door, fronts on the asphalt farm road; in former times the entrance was at the back of the house, which looks onto Varner Creek—then the sole tie to civilization—and which has the same tall pillars and gallery, or porch, at each floor. The cupola was not just decoration but a lookout across the flat country. To the far left in the kitchen wing, the double-throated chimney of the earliest part of the house is so fashioned that a mammoth iron bell can swing in it as a signal to the field hands. It was bought in Galveston in 1859 for $52; the bill survives. *All photographs by Pete Vazquez.*

History in houses

BY ELIZABETH MORFORD

The Varner-Hogg plantation in Texas

LOCATED NEAR WEST COLUMBIA, an hour's drive from Houston, the Varner-Hogg plantation house was built on an 1824 grant from the Mexican government of a league of prairie—some 4,500 acres—which became a tremendous sugar plantation between 1835 and 1860. The first permanent cabin, now part of the kitchen wing, grew into the present galleried two-story house with dependency. Other structures—barns, slave quarters, sugar-boiling sheds, commissaries, race track—have long since gone.

Since construction of the house spanned the period of Mexican rule, the era of the Texas Republic, and the years of the War with Mexico, it is designated a "Texian" residence (an immigrant became a Texian if he settled in the area before Texas came into the United States, a Texan thereafter).

Its location on Varner Creek, then navigable to the Brazos River and thence to the Gulf of Mexico, gave it access by water to Galveston, New Orleans, and the United States. Hogsheads of sugar sailed out; dressed planks and mahogany furniture came back. There were

no overland roads other than Indian trails but weekly sailings to Gulf and Federal ports were scheduled, and by the 1840's the tourist and immigrant traffic was so brisk that passenger steamers with cabins and good cuisine made daily runs from Galveston up the bayous.

The buildings are gray stucco over brick, with white wood trim. The brick was slave-made on the site, of pink Brazos mud and lime from the Gulf oyster beds. Cypress timber for the interior moldings and mantels was brought in from Louisiana, as little suitable wood was available on the prairie.

The plan of the big house, with a chimney at each end and two-story galleries front and rear, is that of the typical Texas country house of the first half of the nineteenth century. The interior is partitioned on each floor into two square rooms connected by an equally large stair hall—an arrangement that gave the rooms three outside exposures and the cross ventilation needed in a sultry climate, while the porches provided shade.

One of the few remaining plantation structures in this area dating as far back as the short span of the

This view of the stair hall shows the typical manner of fastening shut the great double-doors of the house— a removable timber fitted into angle irons in the doorjamb: an essential protection against the yearly threat, not of friendly Ceni Indians, but of tropical hurricane winds. A portrait of Stephen F. Austin, colonizer, hangs above the sofa and is flanked by fac-similes of the land grant he obtained for Martin Varner, the first owner; this parchment gave Varner a three-mile square of prairie provided he built a cabin, started plowing a crop, agred to obey Mexican law, and joined the Catholic Church. On the other walls are framed documents, portraits, and memorabilia relating to the colonizers of Texas. An engraving of Sam Houston hangs to the left of the doorway; beyond is the parlor with its Brussels carpet and a portrait of Sallie Stinson Hogg, the governor's wife. The classic molding detail of the door frame is as elaborate as any found in this section and the bead-and-board paneling under the dado is typical of the locality, while the reveal of the doorway shows the thickness of even the interior walls of the house.

Company sat in the parlor on Belter chairs and sofa to discuss the latest volume published about the colony: Mary Austin Holley's *Texas*, lying open on the rococo center table. On the shelves of the classic revival secretary are firsthand accounts of early travelers to Texas: Mathilda Houstoun of London, the Abbé Domenech, and others who told with gusto of the mud and the biting northers —and also of the number of important houses filled with fine furniture and sound libraries. A portrait of Governor Hogg, whose ownership preserved the house, hangs between the windows.

Like most rooms in Texas houses of the period, the downstairs bedroom has an outside door. The bedspread, a choice example of hooked-and-clipped candlewicking, is one of the many heirlooms associated with the house; the mahogany wardrobe to the left of the fireplace takes the place of a closet. The prints on the wall, the Staffordshire *Franklin* on the far table, the French bisque *Washington* and *Franklin* on the Empire center table, the ormolu Washington clock on the mantel, and the Leeds transfer-printed pitchers flanking it, are the sort of American-historical items popular in the 1820's and 1830's. The Texians were in the main solid, patriotic citizens, in spite of the opinion sometimes expressed that the state was "the great penitentiary where outlaws . . . resort": in the 1830's Mrs. Holley testified that "General Austin never admitted to his colony any man of known disreputable standing."

The floor of this upper bedroom is covered with loomed rag carpeting reproducing what originally lay there. The bed with its high, heavy posts was made in Texas for a neighboring plantation. All the windows are fitted with their old inside folding shutters, to temper the glare and yet admit a draft of air and to give privacy from the second-story gallery when it was made down with pallet beds for visitors. On the washstand are the toilet articles, and in the foreground (to be removed immediately after use) is the portable tin tub. The corner writing desk in late classic revival style, the Victorian rococo easy chairs, the cradle, spell homey comfort and elegance. Propped against the mantel is a numbered Enfield rifle made in 1861-1862 at the short-lived armory at Tyler, Texas.

Republic and one whose acres have been in continuous production—first sugar cane, then cotton, now oil—the house needed only renovation to make it serve as a diary of Texas history; each room presents a chapter. After study of printed and manuscript letters, journals, and travel books written in and about Texas during the years of its colonization, the house has been fitted out with what is believed to be the probable and plausible furniture. That so fine and so stylish a residence as this existed is well attested by travelers' written surprise at

finding its like in the wilderness of huts, mud, shoulder-high grass, and mosquitoes they describe.

The plantation in its middle years became the property of the first native-born Texas governor, and as his home it has survived. Now furnished in the period of 1830-1850 and housing in cases the documents and memorabilia of James Stephen Hogg and the other statesmen who shaped the state, it has been given by Governor Hogg's daughter, Miss Ima, to the Texas Park Board as a historical gallery of the Texian scene.

In another bedroom the bed, of a different southern type, has spindled head and foot of the same height to support at night the mandatory mosquito bar; fitted to a frame, it hung suspended from the ceiling. Engravings flanking the swan-neck bureau are two of a set depicting Champ d'Asile, the abortive encampment established in 1818 by Napoleonic exiles, with the help of the pirate Lafitte, a hundred miles east of here. The fine Brussels carpeting, the rosewood dressing table carved like wooden lace, the claw-foot pedestal card table, the Empire gilt coffee service of French porcelain, the china toilet set are examples of the best to be bought in New Orleans when the crop was sold; indeed, the dressing table and an *étagère* across the room are by the cabinetmaker Prudent Mallard of that city.

In the kitchen wing beyond the covered porch the dining room shows another sort of regional paneling—the high wainscot. In the furniture by Seignouret of New Orleans, the swept line of the back stile of the chairs forms almost a trade mark of his work. Less often seen and identified are his case pieces: the china cabinet here is one. The extension table, of a type often used on plantations, is set with green *Texian Campaigne* plates and tureen, more of which are in the cupboard. Above an American Empire sideboard with carved corner columns, high back, and brass rails, hangs a portrait of General Zachary Taylor, hero of the "Campaigne," and framed Curriers illustrate his winning battles. While homemade candles lighted most rooms, ship chandlers in Galveston regularly stocked whale oil for use in the chandeliers of planters' company rooms.

When the big house was built, out-of-style things that had come down from the States with the family—comfortable windsors and a plank-top table—accumulated in the old storeroom, which became th farm office. On the prominent "New Map" Texas includes present-day New Mexico and Colorado. The design of the quilt hanging at the right shows scenes in the life of Zachary Taylor. Beyond the doorway is the cooking fireplace of the mammoth brick-floored kitchen, so large that the twenty-foot sawbuck table appears as a foreshortened corner. Above it, silhouetted against the window, are mallard duck ready for plucking.

BY CLAY LANCASTER

Fads in nineteenth-century

Iranistan an Oriental Ville (near Bridgeport, Connecticut) The Country seat of P. T. Barnum Esq. Proprietor of the American Museum, New York; lithograph by Sarony and Major.

BY THE YEAR 1800, AMERICAN ARCHITECTURE already had shown signs of experiencing a change from the colonial style borrowed from Georgian England. The more robust Greek Revival had just been introduced by Benjamin Henry Latrobe, who also was responsible for some of the earliest Gothic revival designs in this country. With the Italianate a little later, these "revivals" were to persist as the predominant architectural expression up to the time of the Civil War, after which eclecticism ruled until the end of the century. At the same time there was an undercurrent of minor movements more or less divorced from the steady stream of stylistic development. A building appeared as somebody's fancy. Admired, it was reproduced with changes to suit a different set of conditions, and soon led to a rage. Indigenous in origin, these fads are important because they represent some of our most characteristic types of building.

About the only fad in architecture that the eighteenth century could lay claim to was chinoiserie, or "the Chinese taste," an exoticism based upon motifs borrowed from the Far East combined with a few genuine imported articles such as wallpaper, porcelains, and other bric-a-brac brought by the traders from Macao. The Chinese fashion persisted into the nineteenth century as Chippendale railings (a special favorite of Thomas Jefferson's at the University of Virginia, Monticello, and other houses) and pavilions in pleasure gardens, such as that early one which stood on the grounds of the Markoe house in Philadelphia (ANTIQUES, April 1949, p. 296). Curved-roofed "Chinese" summer houses had become so much a part of what the French called *jardins anglo-chinois* that they were built throughout the nineteenth century as an appropriate accompaniment to the landscaping, changing in character from time to time in accordance with the prevailing architectural trend. Thus a pavilion constructed about the middle of the century

American architecture

would be very likely to show a touch of the Gothic revival, and one dating from the 1870's or 1880's might have
the jigsaw trim, open framing, and wide, overhanging
gables relating it to the Swiss-bracketed mode. As a
fad, the "Chinese" was limited to no one section or
decade; but fad it was nevertheless—never attaining the
status of a major style, and although itself absorbing, re-
fusing to be absorbed by any of them.

Another manifestation of orientalism became a typical
fad, restricted to a period of twelve or fourteen years
and to an exclusive group of enthusiasts, but ardently
admired by these few during its brief existence. I speak
of the style known contemporaneously as "Saracenic,"
"Hindoo," or "Mauresque," inspired by the architecture
of the Moslems and easily recognized by its bulbous
domes, baluster columns, and lobated arches. It is entirely possible that inspiration for this style was the
English palace at Brighton remodeled during the early
nineteenth century by various architects, the final 1815 design by John Nash. The first edifice in America to em-
ploy the style consciously was the Bazaar of Mrs. Frances Trollope, built in Cincinnati about 1828 or 1829,
which I have discussed in a monograph (*Magazine of
Art*, March 1950). The Bazaar antedated the other examples by approximately twenty years.

William Ranlett's *The Architect*, published in New
York in 1848, presented the design of a "Persian Villa,"
the same scheme alternately given a Greek exterior. The
New York architect Leopold Eidlitz also dabbled in
eastern designs and had a few Jewish temples to his credit. His most colorful work was the P. T. Barnum villa
constructed at Bridgeport, Connecticut, in 1848. The
architect's chance of becoming famous through this enterprise was slim because the eccentric owner held its
authorship a secret, referring vaguely to a fictitious international competition or making an absurd claim that
it was a copy of the Brighton Palace. It was a three-
storied rectangular pile with wings, adorned with fancy
piazzas on the front and spherical domes on top, with a
fountain and live deer contributing to the romantic il-
lusion. The interior was an engaging medley of marble,
rosewood, painting, tapestry, mirror, porcelain, and gilding, arranged to hide the baser materials of the sus-
taining structure. Christened "Iranistan" (defined as
"Eastern country place"), Barnum's dream of oriental
splendor was short lived, going up in flame and smoke
on December 18, 1857, with a loss of $150,000 according
to his own estimate.

The most individualistic fad in American architecture
of the nineteenth century was one not of style, but of
shape; and that shape was octagonal. The source of this
vogue is clear and well known. It is traceable to a book
entitled *A Home for All; or, the Gravel Wall and Octagon Mode of Building*, written by the phrenologist Orson
Squire Fowler and published by him in New York in

"Longwood," Natchez, Mississippi. Such orientalized creations were
produced by Henry Austin of New Haven during the latter 1840's
and 1850's, by Samuel Sloan of Philadelphia during the 1850's, and by
Alexander J. Davis of New York City during the fifties and sixties.

brick walls, which entailed additional craftsmen's fees for adjusting right-angle materials to 135-degree corners.

The most famous of octagonal houses was Fowler's own at Fishkill, New York, featured in the builder's book. A towering structure of three stories over a full-height ground story containing the entrance and service rooms, surrounded by piazzas and capped by a glazed belvedere over the central open-newel stairway, the form was imitated throughout America during the decade after the publication of *A Home for All*. Some were moderate-cost versions with simple trim. A resplendent example is Longwood at Natchez, which combined the Moorish fad with the octagonal. To be seen also on the lower Mississippi, and along its tributaries, are a few survivals of another fad of about the same period whose source of inspiration was the design of the ornate packets that plied

Cottage at Nahant, Massachusetts, remodeled by Putnam and Tilden. *Portfolio Club*, The Sketch Book, Boston, 1873, No. VI, pl. 23.

the Mississippi. The decks of these steamboats lent themselves easily to adoption as American verandas; bowed fronts and belvederes (pilothouses) on top required slightly more effort. A few examples (two in the vicinity of New Orleans, for instance) even resorted to metal instead of masonry chimneys. Like many of the other fads in architecture, the steamboat type combined with more widely accepted styles. Hill Forest at Aurora, Indiana, is Italianate, with quoins, Tuscan columns, wide eaves, and arcuated windows and doors. The lightness of its construction (the exterior walls are wood) is decidedly nautical.

The term "steamboat-Gothic" has come into our vocabulary to designate a decorative style of the last half of the nineteenth century which appeared in houses whose shapes had nothing to do with boats, and which is therefore distinguishable from the river valley type described above. Like frosting on a cake, the stylistic overlay could be applied to an early structure of barn simplicity, as was the case with a cottage at Nahant, Massachusetts, remodeled by Putnam and Tilden. The inset shows the house as it appeared prior to the changes of 1872. The roof was extended three feet (secured from high winds with iron rods) and the one-half- to five-eighths-inch openwork on the gables depicted animated local scenes in the various panels: herons bathing, a bear (?) lobstering, a dog hunting; over the kitchen door was an amusing fox banquet. On the first-floor porch, prosaic lattice-work framed openings of unusual shapes. Leaning against the principal spire, a youthful pair tooted toy trumpets.

The very colonial architecture that at Nahant was concealed, elsewhere a decade later was to be resurrected at a high price. McKim, Mead and White's "Colonial tour" of 1877 led to America's most enthusiastic and enduring fad. A house by Chamberlin and Whidden shows the typical result of this vogue, which during the first half of the twentieth century was to overwhelm us with examples poor in both aesthetics and authenticity. The monumental driveway is pure ostentation. The four-paned sash, the coupled windows with shutters (folded under on the outer extremities) are as ugly as they are new; and the balance of these by a Palladian motif over an *oeil-de-boeuf* (presumably lighting a stairway and the w.c. below) was unheard of in the original architecture that this attempts to imitate. The heavy posts of the railing over the entrance porch, the squat dormers, the Chippendale widow's walk, the quoins, entablature, and balcony—all show a speaking acquaintance with the colonial idiom, although the mode of combination leaves much to be desired.

A fervor localized in New York City, for genuine Eastern carving to be incorporated, both inside and outside, in city houses, was personally sponsored by Lockwood de Forest, whose own apartment at 9 East 17th Street was lined with woodwork produced in northern India. In his book of 1885, *Indian Domestic Architecture* (virtually a catalogue of purchasable patterns), he says: "It rests with us . . . whether we are going to allow arts to die out which have taken centuries, with all the advantages [sic] of the caste system of the East, to bring to perfection." A seventeenth-century balcony at Ahmedabad—plate II in the book—was reproduced in India for a bay window on his house at 7 East 10th Street; it substantiates the enthusiasts claim that quality carving could still be executed in India.

American building at the end of the nineteenth century was generally of two main types: the conservative, based upon an eclecticism made up of a number of historic styles, conspicuous among which was French Renaissance; and the liberal, deriving from the English Queen Anne style, Continental *art nouveau,* and our new association with Japan. The confusion created by the coming together of so many elements was tremendous, and one looks for an expression of a single theme as a welcome relief. It can be found in strict imitations of house types developed in mountainous regions all over the world. These included a Norwegian house (Joseph Everett Chandler, architect) at Chestnut Hill, Newton, Massachusetts; a Singhalese villa (shipped from a tea plantation in Ceylon for the Chicago Fair of 1893) on Lake Geneva, Wisconsin; the Japanese house of a Unitarian minister at Fall River, Massachusetts (dismantled circa 1898 when the owner moved to Japan); and a Swiss chalet in Cincinnati, Ohio.

The Swiss chalet was introduced at mid-century through a design in Andrew Jackson Downing's *The Architecture of Country Houses,* and the example illustrated is the highwater mark of the style in America. Although modest in size from the street front, the house, on a hillside site, rises five stories above the terrace at the back. Inside, the main living hall extends up into the second floor. The boldly projecting brackets and exquisite carving around the upper part of the house suggest that the woodwork may have been produced in Switzerland, where the architect maintained social and commercial connections.

The fads of the 1800's not only give character and variety to our architecture: they have a deeper significance as the embodiment of the taste, ideas, and ideals of nineteenth-century America. They signify at once her internationalism and her creativity. Although we smile at their eccentricity, we recognize in them a note of freshness and enterprise that we admire; and we accept them as part of the wonderful cultural complexity that is our heritage.

Seventeenth-century carving on a balcony at Ahmedabad. *Plate II, Indian Domestic Architecture, by Lockwood De Forest.*

Reproduction of above on a house occupied by Mr. De Forest at 7 East 10th Street. *Photograph by the author.*

Swiss chalet built for A. D. Fisher by architect Lucien F. Plympton in Walnut Hills, Cincinnati, Ohio, in 1892; now the home of the director of the Cincinnati Art Museum. The Inland Architect and News Record, *Vol. XXVIII, January, 1897.*

Roseland, a Gothic Revival mansion

A picket fence in the same pattern as the porch columns divides Roseland from the street. Andrew Jackson Downing, the great champion of the Gothic, felt that a modified version of this style, what he called the Rural Gothic or Tudor, "with high gables, wrought with tracery, bay windows, and other features full of domestic expression," was the best choice for a private house. By contrast to the contemporary Italianate styles, for example, that suggested "the gay spirit of the drawing room and social life," the Gothic seemed to him to speak of "quiet domestic feeling and the family circle." The Gothic house should have—as Roseland does— "secluded shadowy corners . . . nooks where one would love to linger . . . cozy rooms where fireside joys are invited to dwell." *Photographs by James C. Ward.*

BY RUTH DAVIDSON

The Marquis de Chastellux, who traveled in Connecticut in 1781 and 1782, wrote that he was "particularly struck with the position of Woodstock-meeting, which is placed on an eminence, commanding a very gay and well-peopled country." A house erected more than half a century later on one side of the irregular green of what is now West Woodstock would have heightened this happy impression. It is Roseland, a Gothic Revival mansion named for the extensive rose gardens that once surrounded it and now known to many thereabouts as the Pink House. For Roseland has in fact always been painted a bright, cheerful pink, with its ornamental bargeboards, crockets, and pinnacles, its oriel window and trellised porches picked out in dark red—a combination of colors that make blue skies and the green and gold of foliage seem more vivid.

Gothic Revival houses are still not extremely rare in New England, though their numbers are being depleted at a frightening rate. But few have been as well preserved as Roseland, or as lovingly maintained by successive generations of the same family down to the present. And fewer still have as much of their original furni-

"Carpenter Gothic," as it is sometimes called, simulating medieval ornament in wood, achieves its own distinctive and pleasing character through the use of vertical sheathing and scroll-sawn bargeboards, crockets, and trellises. At Roseland these details are painted dark red to contrast with the pink of the house. The gable end set parallel to the street and flanked by porches is a feature also of the Rotch house in New Bedford by A. J. Davis, among other examples. This view shows the porte-cochere at the main entrance; the chimney stacks, made of glazed pink stoneware molded in Gothic designs; and the quatrefoil pattern of the pierced porch columns, a motif repeated in the carved decoration of the parlor furniture. The Woodstock elms are famous.

Front and back parlors, identical in plan, open off the central hall, taking up the side of the house parallel to the street. Each has a deep bay window at one end and a door leading into the conservatory between the two porches. This picture shows the end of the back parlor, with one of the two window seats designed, like the set of matching chairs and settee, by the architect of the house. Frosted diamond-shape panes of red, blue, gold, green, and violet glass, set in mullioned casements, let the light through in Gothic diaper patterns or heraldic designs. The glass is thought to be American.

In the front parlor a typically mid-nineteenth-century arrangement puts the marble-topped octagonal pedestal table and two flanking chairs, one an upholstered Grecian form and the other, part of the carved Gothic set, in the center of the room, facing the Italian carved marble mantel. Ceramic tiles of a later date surround the fireplace opening and cover the hearth. On the mantel, beneath a family portrait, is a set of candelabra with bases of cast, gilded metal in the form of a Turkish lady—reminding us, like the Turkish brass scimitar and bowl on the table, that the Gothic Revival was only one aspect of Victorian eclecticism. On a second marble-topped table, at the right of the fireplace, is a collection of family memorabilia and *souvenirs de voyage* that includes a Turkish mosque lamp, some fine miniatures, and a piece of pottery presented to a member of the family by Mme. Heinrich Schliemann, wife of the excavator of ancient Troy.

The settee from the set of furniture that matches the window seat is shown here beneath a steel engraving of Windsor Castle. The marble-topped stand exemplifies what was called in its day Elizabethan furniture. (See Robert C. Smith's article on this revival style in ANTIQUES, March 1959, p. 272.) French doors at the left open on to the trellised porch. Near them, though not visible in our picture, stands an Aaron Willard table clock, an heirloom, like the fine Hepplewhite chest of drawers in the upper hall, that held its place in spite of the fashion for Gothic. The heavily embossed wallpaper in both parlors, dark green on a cream-color ground, was made in England in the 1860's; *Lincrusta Walton* was the name of the pattern.

A particularly arresting architectural detail is the arched passage between the front and back parlors. Two closets and two sliding doors are contained in the partition. All the doors and the soffit of the arch, like the rest of the woodwork on the ground floor, are grained to simulate light oak. The doors are actually carved in pointed, trifoliated Gothic arches, but the soffit is painted in *trompe l'oeil* to give the same effect. The gilded eagle that topped the flagpole on the lawn when Henry Bowen celebrated the Fourth of July now has its eyrie here. Throughout the house the doorknobs are ceramic, marbled blue and white.

ture. Many such houses were probably furnished by their first owners with a mixture of Gothic, Grecian, and hand-me-down, and Gothic furniture, never made here in great quantity, is scarce today. Roseland, however, still has the furniture designed for its double parlor by the architect of the house and repeating, in its carved decoration, the quatrefoils and foliated arches of the exterior trim.

The architect was Joseph C. (?) Wells of New York, who was also responsible for the First Presbyterian Church, erected in 1846 on Fifth Avenue between Eleventh and Twelth Streets. His client was Henry Chandler Bowen (1813-1896), a successful merchant, one of the founders of *The Independent* and, later, sole owner of the paper. Roseland Park, Woodstock's fine wooded recreational area, was presented to the town by Henry Bowen in 1876. He also inaugurated the Woodstock Fourth of July celebrations that for fifty years attracted nationwide attention because of the prominence of the speakers. At the Woodstock celebration in 1877 Oliver Wendell Holmes read two poems composed for the occasion. In one of these, *A Family Record*, he evokes the memory of his own Woodstock ancestor, Dr. David Holmes, who served as a surgeon in the French and Indian and Revolutionary Wars. But many in his audience had even older ties with the town. Henry Bowen himself was a descendant of that earlier Henry Bowen who with twelve other "planters," or potential plantation holders, was sent out from Roxbury, Massachusetts, in 1686 to "spy out" and take actual possession of the land for the new town of Woodstock.

Wabbaquasset ("mat-producing place") was the Indian name of the village closest to the present site of Woodstock. It was part of the Nipmuck or fresh-water country that was divided, for missionary purposes, into Praying Villages. John Eliot preached there in 1674. The old "Connecticut Path," for long the route of settlers leaving Massachusetts to found new towns, the vital link between the Connecticut colonies and the Massachusetts Bay settlements, passed through what is now Woodstock. Judge Samuel Sewall gave the town its name in 1689/90 "because of its nearness to Oxford [Woodstock is about as close to Oxford, Massachusetts, as the royal hunting park and lodge were to the English university town] . . . and the notable meetings that have been held at the place bearing the name in England."

As Clarence Winthrop Bowen, compiler of the monumental *Woodstock Genealogies*, pointed out in an address read on the occasion of the bicentennial (1886), the new-world Woodstock has kept up that tradition of "notable meetings." The town has been host to all the Presidents from Grant to McKinley. Hayes, Harrison, Cleveland, and McKinley were overnight guests at Roseland, occupying the spacious upstairs suite still referred to as the Pink Room. Ulysses S. Grant, who was also invited to Woodstock by Henry Bowen and State Senator Buckingham, did not spend the night, but after lunching at Roseland he enjoyed the bowling alley behind the house. The President made a ten-strike but declined a second ball and walked out lighting a "segar." The bowling alley, still standing ready for use with its old equipment, may be one of the earliest surviving examples in the country. It is attached to the gabled carriage house, which has ornamental bargeboards like the mansion, and the whole long structure is painted the same pink with maroon trim.

But the name of Woodstock has still more associations

A substantial marble-topped sideboard in the neoclassical style has always stood in the house and probably always looked as much at home as it does now, since Gothic and Grecian furniture seem to have been freely mixed in houses of the period. On the sideboard is part of a Limoges porcelain dinner service with deep rose-color borders and the initials *HCB* in gold; it was made in France for Henry Chandler Bowen. The painting is evidently an old copy of the head of Stuart's *Washington at Dorchester Heights*.

The oriel visible in our exterior view (beneath the front gable, between the two trellised porches) lights a small room on the upper floor and provides an enticing window seat. The "cottage furniture," of the type specifically recommended by Downing for bedrooms in country houses, is painted red with line decoration in gold. Reflected in the mirror at right is an unusual stepped semicircular console table.

for us than it had for Samuel Sewall, and as we enter Henry Bowen's mansion by the castellated porte-cochere under a heraldic shield, or, sitting in one of the deep bay windows of the parlors, watch the light that comes through the colored glass windowpanes tracing Gothic diapers on floor and walls, we may be put in mind of the "ancient and venerable turrets, bearing each its own vane of rare device," and the "antique apartments," with their trophies and massive fireplaces, that Sir Walter Scott described in his novel *Woodstock*. This is what the architect of Roseland and his client would have wished. With the growing appreciation of nineteenth-century romantic architecture it has come to be realized that the eclecticism of the period is due, on the whole, not to lack of inventiveness but to what Wayne Andrews defines as an attempt to introduce into building "the fourth dimension, time itself." Like the Grecian and other revival styles, the "Gothick," of which Roseland is such a compelling example, represents, in his words, "so many efforts to explore the poetry of time."

In one of the upstairs bedrooms a porcelain figure of a Balkan mountaineer in melting pastel colors stands on a rococo base in the same shades. Such decorations remind us again that the taste for Gothic did not exclude Turkish, Moorish, or Swiss, any more than it did Grecian ornament. This piece is probably of French origin.

The extensive gardens that suggested Roseland's name have given way to more restricted plantings within box hedges, but the little garden house in the form of a pedimented Greek temple still stands beside the Gothic mansion—another example of the mixture of revival styles.

History in houses

Fountain Elms in Utica, New York

BY RICHARD B. K. MC LANATHAN, *Director, Munson-Williams-Proctor Institute*

Fountain Elms. The main block is substantially as it was in 1850; the ell in back represents various periods of remodeling.

THE RESTORATION OF A nineteenth-century Tuscan villa presented most of the problems but many more documentary solutions than are usually found in houses of an earlier period. With the aid of the original architectural drawings and the family papers and library, Fountain Elms has been restored as accurately as possible to its 1850 appearance. The resulting combination of color and design with objects from far and near is somewhat remote from today's taste, yet manages to recapture the atmosphere of a century ago—of a world bustling with vigor, self-confidence, and gusto.

The mansion was built in 1850 after the designs of an Albany architect, William J. Woollett Jr., by builder Philip Thomas of Utica. It was the gift of Alfred Munson to his daughter Helen Elizabeth and her husband, James Watson Williams. Williams was his own superintending architect, supplied the design for the fountain in front of the house (see top of Contents page), and completed the project with a gazebo and gardens, and with interior furnishings of taste and elegance. The young couple had two daughters, Maria and Rachel, who grew up in Fountain Elms and later married two brothers, Thomas Redfield and Frederick Towne Proctor, from Proctor-

ville, Vermont; the Frederick Proctors lived in the house for many years until it was inherited in 1935 by the Munson-Williams-Proctor Institute, founded in 1919 by the Thomas Proctors and Frederick Proctor. The villa is an important part of the institute, which also includes a community art school and a recently completed museum building designed by Philip Johnson.

Many changes had been made in the house since 1850; a small two-story wing had been added to the north, and a series of additions and changes had been made to the ell. In the interior, diagonal partitions had been removed to throw the drawing room and dining room together, the original ground-floor bedroom had become the dining room, and all the fireplaces had been changed. Since it seemed impractical to demolish the various additions in view of the institute's need for all possible space, it was decided to restore the four major rooms on the ground floor and the hall as accurately as possible to their original appearance, using the architectural drawings which had been preserved, following evidence of family papers, bills, letters, and inventories, and referring to books on art, architecture, gardening, and furnishing, acquired by Williams at the time the house was planned. A side porch, incorporating the remains of an original porch and adding a terrace—both based on designs from architectural books in Williams' library—was completed.

Though many fragments of carpeting, upholstery and drapery materials, and wallpapers were found, it was impossible to obtain sufficient quantities in good enough condition for the restoration, so that all the carpets and wallpapers and most of the fabrics had to be reproductions. The original carpets were English, purchased from A. T. Stewart and Company in New York, and most if not all of the other materials were also imported, so that through the assistance of many, but especially of the Cooper Union Museum and the Victoria and Albert Museum, we discovered original designs of the 1840's which were checked against our records. The carpets were woven by an English firm (a successor to one which had exported to America in the 1840's), using designs of the mid-nineteenth century. They were produced according to contemporary specifications, with special dyeing and twisting of yarn in the narrow widths required by the old looms, and were sewn and laid in the manner of the period. Upholstery and drapery materials and wallpapers were accurately reproduced following contemporary samples of local provenance, wherever possible.

In the hallway, the stenciled rosewood and marble table with matching chairs, c. 1830, is from the Randall mansion in Cortland, New York. The gilt mirror of the same period bears the label of Isaac Platt, New York City, and is from the same house. Family taste in art is reflected in the portraits of General and Mrs. Jacob Brown of Brownville, New York, attributed to Ezra Ames (1768-1836), and the marble bust of Alfred Munson by Erastus Dow Palmer (1817-1904), who had a studio in Albany for over twenty-five years after 1846.

The marble statue of a boy fisherman across the hall is a portrait of Rhinelander Waldo of New York, commissioned of Carelli in Florence about 1850. Hanging at the head of the stairs is a portrait of Andrew Dexter and his sister Mary Frances of Whitesboro by Alvah Bradish (1806-1901), painted about 1835. Colors in the hallway are rich and complement the black and gold of the furniture: brown and gold wallpaper after a design by Pugin, carpet in red, gold, and green.

The front hall floor was laid in Dutch and New York State tile, similar to that in the dated hall pavement of Lorenzo, a house in Cazenovia, New York. Woodwork in the hall, painted in medium and dark tones of gray and brown, follows local and other contemporary examples, the "stone colors" recommended by Andrew Jackson Downing, several of whose books were in the library of Fountain Elms. The *Journal of Design and Manufacture*, six volumes published in connection with the Great Exhibition of 1851, which were bought by Williams as they were issued between 1849 and 1852, were invaluable for many purposes, but especially for checking color, as the samples of original papers and textiles which they contain have been largely preserved from fading.

Chandeliers and lamps were acquired, with but few exceptions, from contemporary New York State houses, though many were of European as well as American manufacture. The original fixtures, long since removed, had been purchased from the mid-nineteenth-century firms of J. Stouvenal and Company, 594 Broadway, and Haughwout and Daily, 561 and 563 Broadway, New York City, with a few supplied by William Munsig of Albany. Hardware for doors, including "Hispaniolet barrs," fortunately almost entirely preserved, had been supplied by Theodore Russell of New York City. The modern fireplaces were replaced with contemporary examples representing the taste of the area, white marble for the drawing room and black for the dining room as specified in Williams' letter to the architect.

Furniture includes family pieces inherited by the institute, pieces of regional origin or ownership, or those

that follow regional precedent. Many, including a drawing room set by Belter and examples by Galusha, Phyfe, and Quervelle, are signed, labeled, or otherwise documented. There are sculptures by Hiram Powers, Erastus Dow Palmer, and others; paintings, including family portraits, by such artists as Ezra Ames, Thomas Hicks, Jasper F. Cropsey, Joshua Shaw, Henry Darby, and Saint-Mémin; engravings by leading artists of the first half of the nineteenth century include a proof set by Smillie after Thomas Cole's famous *Voyage of Life* paintings, long in the possession of St. Luke's Hospital and now in the institute's collection. Silver, porcelain, and other objects, many of them family possessions, are mostly European.

Today Fountain Elms again reflects the security and elegance of the 1850's. It recaptures the atmosphere of a community to which the canal system had brought great prosperity, and whose solid citizens read in their daily papers the exciting news of gold in far-off California and of the latest industrial and artistic wonders at the Crystal Palace exhibition in London.

Niches on either side of the doorway between parlor and dining room were restored in the remodeling and have been appropriately filled with marble figures by Thomas Crawford (1814-1857), on loan to the institute; shown here is a little dancing girl. The *étagère* and two chairs are by Galusha.

The deep red of the damask draperies, made in the 1830's for the Joseph Bonaparte house in Bordentown, New Jersey, dominates the dining room. Of the same period are the stenciled table, probably a New York City piece, made for a Syracuse family, and the New York State sideboard. Above the sideboard is a portrait by Ezra Ames (1768-1836) of Ann Varick, of a prominent Utica family. The English silver coffee urn and candelabra are Williams family pieces, as are the stenciled Biedermeier chairs from the collection of Otto Meyer, an early benefactor of the institute. The chandelier was made about 1850 by Cornelius and Baker of Philadelphia, who produced an enormous pair for the Great Exhibition of 1851. Flocked wallpaper and the gold, brown, and green carpet are reproductions.

The opposite dining-room wall has a black marble mantel with cast-iron inset which came from a local house of the same period as Fountain Elms. The style of the mantel suggests that it might have been used before that in an earlier house. The pair of console tables flanking the fireplace are probably New England, c. 1820, though long owned by a New York family. Above the fireplace hangs an elaborate English gilt mirror from a house in Herkimer, New York; the clock below is French, and the Argand lamps on either side were made in Philadelphia and purchased in 1832 for a house in Brooklyn. An elegant black and gilt coal scuttle of New York provenance sits near the hearth. Portraits by Frederick R. Spencer (1806-1875) are of Joseph Kirkland, first mayor of Utica, and his wife, and the crayon portrait by Saint-Mémin (1770-1852) is of Gerrit Boon of Barneveld, New York, purchasing agent for the Holland Land Company. The Continental porcelains are Williams family pieces.

In the library is a gilded mahogany
Empire secretary, bearing the label of
Anthony G. Quervelle of Philadelphia
and dating from c. 1830, which has
been owned in Utica for over a century. It was first published in *Queries
and Opinions* in ANTIQUES, November 1934, p. 195. The portrait of
Michael Moore, proprietor of Moore's
Hotel, Trenton Falls, New York, a
favorite resort of artists and writers,
was painted by Thomas Hicks (1823-
1890) in 1858, and is flanked by a
small pair of portraits of James Watson Williams, who built the house, and
his wife, by Henry F. Darby (1831-?).
The mantel of white marble, marble-
ized in brown and black, is of local
origin; the whale-oil lamps on the
mantel were made by Johnson Brookes
of London and sold by Bemis and
Vose of Boston. A pair of bookcases,
made in the 1840's for the Gothic
cottage on Nicholas Biddle's estate,
Andalusia, are filled with books from
the Williams library.

The gilded black table, c. 1830, an
outstanding piece of japan work combining French, Gothic, and Chinese
motifs, is of New York origin, and
above it hangs a handsome black and
gilt gas chandelier of 1850 made in
Philadelphia. The writing table and
chair are Williams family pieces. The
looped-pile carpet in black and brown
is a reproduction of an English design of the 1840's, as is the purple
wallpaper, a flocked stripe. Green
velvet draperies with green and gold
tassels were copied from a decorator's
book of the period. On either side
of the window hang crayon portraits
by Thomas Bluget de Valdenuit
(1763-1846) of George Clinton, first
governor of New York, and his wife.

362

ANTIQUES

The variety of styles in mid-Victorian furniture is especially well illustrated in the downstairs bedroom. A Renaissance rosewood bureau by Galusha stands beside a delicate rococo lady's desk of rosewood with inlay, c. 1850, which has the stamp of F. W. Hutchings of New York City (Hutchings sold the Williamses several pieces). A third style is represented by the "Turkish" chair, one of two in the bedroom—a New York piece of similar date. Across the room is a massive Empire bed veneered in fiddle-back mahogany, c. 1840, from Glen, New York, and a bronze-mounted bureau in the same style, c. 1835. A richly carved marble fireplace, c. 1845, from a house in Canandaigua, New York, exhibits a Jacob Petit porcelain garniture. The table in the center of the room is by Belter and the chair, unusual in its carved decoration, is American, probably made for a house in Maine. The gilt-bronze French chandelier with gaily painted glass shades came from a New York State house. Both carpet and wallpaper are based on designs of the 1840's, the carpet English and the wallpaper French. Hangings on the bed and at the windows are copies of originals in the institute's collection from an 1847 house in Auburn, New York. (The bed hangings, photographed before completion, are now edged with braid, like the curtains.)

For other illustrations, see color insert.

ARCHITECTURAL TRADITIONS OF NEW YORK

By LORING McMILLEN

The chief avocation of Mr. McMillen, whose vocation is with the New York Telephone Company, is the study of architecture, and he is now gathering material for a book on early construction methods. As Director of the Staten Island Historical Society's museum, he has a particular interest in New York architecture.

THERE ARE FEW SECTIONS of our country where the traditional architecture is less understood than in the section embraced by the former Dutch colony of New Netherland. This section extended from the Connecticut River on the east to the Delaware River on the south, and north to the city of Albany, thus including parts of the present states of Delaware, New Jersey, New York, and Connecticut. By the time of the English conquest in 1664, however, the Dutch influence was restricted to the Hudson and Mohawk River valleys and a section now known as the metropolitan area of New York City, which includes a portion of New Jersey.

Many causes contribute to this misunderstanding. One is the almost total destruction of the earlier traditional architectural examples throughout the area, particularly in New York City. Another is the lack of published material dealing exclusively and analytically with the subject. Other causes lie in the history of the region, which embraces many diversified nationalities.

New Netherland was settled not only by the Dutch but by the French, Germans, and English as well. During the first generation at least, each nationality built in the only style it

FIG. 1—TRADITIONAL DUTCH HOUSE *(seventeenth century)*. In Leyden, Holland. *Except as noted, photographs by the author.*

knew, the traditional style of the homeland. Thus we find many styles at first: the stepped gabled brick house of the Dutch, the low stone house with simple high gable of the French and Germans, and the hewn frame or half-timbered house of the English.

One of the most picturesque styles of architecture ever brought to our shores by any of our first European colonists was the true, or traditional, Dutch colonial *(Fig. 2)*. This style is characterized by a compact, proportionately tall building of brick, surmounted by a characteristic medieval gable in which the wall was carried above the roof surface and terminated in a coping parallel with the slope of the roof or in corbeled or "crow" steps, as they were called. The peak was flat and surmounted by a weather vane, the maintenance of which is said to account for the steps. The bricks along this coping were often laid in a saw-toothed pattern called in Dutch *muizentanden* (mouse teeth). Contrary to tradition, bricks were made locally, as is proved by abundant contemporary evidence. Brick was the traditional Dutch building material, since both stone and timber were scarce in Holland. However, with a tradition of shipbuilding behind them, the Dutch produced a house which was in reality a hewn frame mortised and tenoned and pinned together, around and between which the bricks were laid, giving the appearance of a brick house. The ornamental iron figures which appear in the gable ends of these houses were the anchor ends which secured the brick walls to the timber frame. Roof surfaces were covered at first with clapboards or thatch, then tiles, and finally wooden shingles.

In the towns of Albany and New York these houses were constructed gable end to the street and rose two and a half or more stories in height. The first floor was occupied by a shop or store and the living quarters were on the second floor. The garret was used for storage. On the farms this type of house was of one story and a half, since no shop on the first floor was necessary, and the entrance usually was on the long side. No symmetry existed in the arrangement of windows or doors. Such buildings were, in reality, a survival from medieval times.

FIG. 2—TRADITIONAL DUTCH COLONIAL HOUSE *(c. 1720)*. House of Hendrick Bries, Rensselaer County, New York. Note steep pitch of roof, handsome iron beam anchors, and "mouse-teeth" pattern of bricks along coping. *Photograph by Margaret De M. Brown, courtesy of The Holland Society.*

FIG. 3—TRADITIONAL DUTCH COLONIAL HOUSE (c. 1680). House of Christopher Billop at Tottenville, Staten Island, New York. Also called the Conference House because here was held the only peace conference between American and British representatives during the Revolution. Combines typical Dutch form with conventional English Renaissance front. Greek Revival veranda has been removed since this picture was taken. *Photograph by Eugene G. Putnam.*

today of the typical Dutch gable in a combination of stone and brick, with the conventional front of an English country house of the Renaissance period (*Fig. 3*). The same is true elsewhere: English influence was found largely in the more pretentious houses which were built in the middle and late eighteenth century. In details such as door and window trim, paneling of doors, and chimney pieces, however, English forms prevailed after the period 1700-1730.

By 1720-1730 these traditional or native European styles had lost most of their individuality. A simple style resulted which we may call the cosmopolitan, usually a stone house, though often brick or frame, one story in the country, two stories in villages or towns, with a low, single-pitched or gambrel roof. The house had little additional embellishment; its charm resulted from a mingling of the various elements of good proportions (*Fig. 5*). It was used throughout the Hudson Valley until after 1800, when such new styles as the Greek Revival began to crowd it out.

This cosmopolitan style which evolved from the traditional forms bears a greater resemblance to the plain French structures than to any other native style, including the Dutch. While it would thus appear that its origin was more French than anything else, its growth and survival were due not so much to any prevailing nationality as to its suitability to the materials at hand, to the severity of the climate, and to the rugged character of the people who had to wrest a living from the soil of a new country.

Simultaneously with this simple style, there were being built more monumental examples by the wealthier families, usually in the prevailing style of the town or country house of England. These were, however, exceptional and only a few exist today, such as the Philipse Manor, Yonkers, and

By 1730 this type of house had ceased to be built. While great numbers once existed, it is a deplorable fact that today not more than ten of these traditional Dutch colonial buildings still survive. Following is a list of these buildings, all in New York State. Three of them are in almost hopeless ruin. Certainly something should be done to preserve the rest.

House of Pieter Bronck (*c. 1662-1669*), West Coxsackie. Good example in stone; roof altered.
Conference House (*c. 1680*), Tottenville, Staten Island. Good example of Dutch gable combined with formal English country house. Owned by the Conference House Association (*Fig. 3*).
Fort Crailo (*c. 1700*), 10 Riverside Avenue, Rensselaer. Restored and owned by the State of New York.
House of Ariaantje Coeymans (*c. 1716*), Coeymans. Splendid example, but altered and in poor repair.
House of Hendrick Bries (*c. 1720*), on the river road below Rensselaer (*Fig. 2*). In ruins.
House of Gerret Vandenbergh (*c. 1720*), Bethlehem (formerly *Domine's Hoeck*), Albany County. In ruins.
Kost Verloren ("Money Thrown Away") or Teller House (*c. 1730*), on river road south of Rensselaer. Good condition, except that typical Dutch roof was altered early to a gambrel.
House of Abraham Yates (*c. 1730*), 109 Union Street, Schenectady. Splendid example in good condition.
Van Allen House (*1737*), near Kinderhook, Columbia County. In ruins.
House of Leendert Bronck (*1738*), West Coxsackie. Good condition.

The contribution to our architecture by the French Huguenots who settled at New Paltz and Staten Island, and in lesser numbers elsewhere, has been overlooked. The plain stone house with the high-pitched steep roof, such as the Jean Hasbrouck House, New Paltz, built in 1712, can be seen dotting the countrysides of France. Examples are found throughout the Hudson Valley and several also stand on Staten Island (*Fig. 4*).

German and English influence in the traditional architecture of New York is not as apparent as the Dutch and French. While at first the English built in their traditional style, as the records indicate at Gravesend, when Christopher Billop built his large mansion house about 1680 at Tottenville, Staten Island, he produced one of the few examples remaining

FIG. 4—TRADITIONAL FRENCH COLONIAL HOUSE (c. 1680). Old Guard House at Hurley, New York, probably the oldest of the type in the region. The jigsaw trimming on the steep roof is a Victorian addition.

the Van Cortlandt Mansion (built 1748), Van Cortlandt Park, New York City, which is illustrated elsewhere in this issue.

Between 1700 and 1740 there began to develop a style which was as much a part of New York as the literature of Washington Irving or the art of the Hudson Valley school became in the following century. And like these cultural expressions, this new style had a warmth and individuality which distinguish it as one of the very few styles to have its beginnings in this country. It has come to bear the misleading name of "Dutch colonial"—misleading since the style had its inception many years after New Netherland had ceased to be a Dutch colony, and a combination of many nationalities had a part in its development. However, for lack of a better name and in deference to the Dutch who were the preponderant nationality, the term, when understood, can be descriptive.

Peculiarly, the "Dutch colonial" was developed only in the metropolitan area of New York and but for a few isolated examples is not found elsewhere. It reached its fullest development about 1780-1790, finally disappearing about 1820-1830. The one feature which distinguishes it from all other styles is the roof, which in the earliest known example—the Voorlezer's House *(1695)*, at Richmond, Staten Island—extended beyond the front wall a distance of 24 inches. A characteristic upward flare was given to this "spring eave," adding greatly to its architectural merit. As the style developed, the extension was carried further and until about 1760-1770 was unsupported. At this time the extension reached a sufficient distance so that supports could be placed at intervals to form a piazza extending the length of the building. Further development placed this piazza at both front and rear *(Fig. 6)*. The most typical roof line was the gambrel although the roof of single pitch was also common. The popularity of this style caused it to be

applied to existing buildings by simply extending the roof.

In fairness to the genesis of this "Dutch colonial" style, it should be stated that along the banks of the St. Lawrence River this same style of spring eave, combined only with a roof of single pitch and never terminating in a piazza, was separately developed by the French Canadians *(Fig. 7)*. Here the style seems to have had a period of use contemporary with that of New York, but no evidence exists as to whether one influenced the other or was copied directly. My personal belief is that these were two curious and entirely separate developments growing out of an inherent instinct for the beautiful common to all people, unlike the development in the south and middle west where the roof was carried down over a piazza in a straight line for the practical purpose of protection from the elements.

Thus we see in the early architectural history of New York the separate styles or phases which are so commonly misunderstood: the several traditional styles of the various nationalities comprising the population, the amalgamation of these styles into a cosmopolitan style with local variations, and the emergence in metropolitan New York alone of the "Dutch Colonial."

Domestic architecture of New Jersey

BY JACK E. BOUCHER

The Shorn log cabin, c. 1675, near Repaupo and Raccoon Creek in Gloucester County. Attributed to a Swedish settler. *Photographs by the author.*

Vaux Hall, near Greenwich, in Cumberland County was built about 1695, and reflects the early Dutch influence in domestic architecture. Paneling from this early residence is installed in the Winterthur Museum in Delaware.

DOMESTIC ARCHITECTURE IS PERHAPS the most graphic reminder of a region's heritage and traditions. Unlike public buildings, which are monuments to their architects, the early private houses were usually designed by builders who lacked formal training, and reflected the personal tastes of owner and builder alike. In New Jersey the distinctive styles of three centuries range from the log cabin of the seventeenth century to the flamboyant Victorian mansions of the nineteenth.

While the Dutch and Flemish influence was felt most heavily in the northern counties, especially bordering on the Hudson River, the Dutch had a pronounced effect also in the Delaware River region of South Jersey. Germanic traditions are reflected in northwestern Jersey, while Swedish and English styles dominate the southern parts of the state.

Geography and the availability of materials were other governing factors. Softwoods (pine and cedar), clay, and sandstone were prime materials in the flat southern portion of the state; hardwoods (oak and poplar) and stone (including Jersey granite, dolomitic limestone, and a reddish-brown sandstone) were favored by builders in the hilly and mountainous northern regions of the state. By the mid-eighteenth century, iron furnaces and forges dotted the province, providing nails and hardware, while glasshouses from Wistarberg (c. 1739) to Batsto (1846 to 1867) provided window glass.

In Cape May County at the southern tip of the state a unique industry of "mined" or "dug" cedar shingles flourished during the nineteenth century. These extremely durable shingles were cut from trees buried in water and mud of swamps thousands of years ago.

Jersey bog ore, a variety of limonite, was another raw material that exerted an unusual architectural influence. In the natural state, a reddish-brown conglomerate stone, it was used in building foundations and for walls, fireplaces, and chimneys as well. Refined in a local blast furnace, it made iron that carried the settlers through life and even death, for the forges produced not only the nails and hardware mentioned, but also ship and wagon and wheel fittings, hollow ware, salt evaporation pans, cannon, shot and ball, and, finally, grave markers.

English settlers in South Jersey left a heritage in brick houses that has been termed "unexcelled and probably unequalled in America." A dozen varieties of brick bonds grace these houses, including English, Flemish, common, heading, stretching, facing, monk, English garden wall, Dutch, Yorkshire flying, Flemish garden wall, English cross. Combinations of these bonds have been used with vitrified brick to create artistic patterns ranging from a simple checkerboard or herringbone to an ornate, even gaudy, diaper pattern. Structures in Salem and Cumberland Counties frequently bear the initials of the builder or owner and the date of construction high on the gable end of the house.

Early Dutch houses in North Jersey were usually single-story structures with a gambrel roof gradually sloping to the lower pitch of less than forty-five degrees, and were built of reddish-brown sandstone (not to be confused with South Jersey's bog-ore conglomerate). South Jersey's Dutch houses were also single story with gambrel roof but generally smaller in floor plan, and the lower pitch to the roof was very steep. They were usually built of brick.

Wooden houses in the early days of the province were often built with a pinned oak framing and elaborate bracing. Brick nogging and frequently employed, sometimes without mortar, as late as the mid-nineteenth century, providing a degree of insulation for the house. The nogging was covered with exterior weatherboarding, either lapped or butted, thus hiding the half-timbered construction. Early weatherboarding was beaded along the exposed weather edge until the early nineteenth century.

Summer beams, running parallel to the end elevation of the house, were frequently used, but were usually concealed. A notable exception is in the Ewing House on Ye Greate Street in Greenwich, where a massive timber parallels the front elevation. Exposed "gunstock cornerposts," often used in South Jersey, are also found in this old house, believed to have been built about the turn of the seventeenth century.

As the population of the state became more cosmopolitan after the Revolution, so did its architecture. Wood became the prime building material for residential

Somers Mansion in Somers Point, overlooking Great Egg Harbor Bay, reflects the style of Vaux Hall, but with distinctive features which include a pent roof on the gabled end. This house, now a state historic site and headquarters of the Atlantic County Historical Society, was built about 1725. Detail shows one of two unusual overdoor ventilators in the living room.

use in South Jersey, while varieties of native stone and imported granite continued in popularity in the northern tier of the state.

A number of small factory villages, parts of which still exist today, came into being about this time. Notable among these are Batsto and Weymouth, both iron-furnace villages, where the workers' houses were of frame construction, two and one-half stories in height, low ceilinged, and simple in plan. Fireplaces and their chimneys were located at one end of the house, and a narrow, board-enclosed stair led to the second floor, next to the fireplace. Walls were plastered, but the ceiling joists were exposed and often beaded.

The houses at Batsto are excellent examples of a type popularly known as Jersey's "black houses." Unlike the typical "Down-Jersey" house, which was weatherboarded in pine and painted, these houses were covered with lapped, narrow, cedar clapboards and never painted, although a very few were whitewashed occasionally. In time, the weather darkened the durable cedar boards to a rich brown-black appearance, giving the houses their nickname.

Estellville, a glassworks hamlet some twenty miles distant, which thrived from 1825 to mid-century, boasted a number of duplex workers' houses. These were frame, two and one-half stories tall, but with a double-flue chimney that served

The Gibbon House in Greenwich was constructed by Nicholas Gibbon about 1730 and is among the earliest houses in South Jersey showing English influence.

The finest example of the use of glazed headers to make an ornate design in a brick wall is in Salem County's Dickinson House, built in 1754 for John and Martha Dickinson. While most houses in the area boast only the initials of the builder or owner and date, possibly with a checkerboard or herringbone pattern, an anonymous mason lavished all his skill and knowledge in producing a pattern of diamonds on this single end wall.

The Elijah Clark Mansion in Pleasant Mills, a rural South Jersey village, c. 1762, is among the earliest remaining frame houses in the region. *Residence of Mr. and Mrs. Raymond Baker.*

a fireplace in each unit. This fireplace was used for cooking as well as heating, and accordingly had built-in cranes.

To the north, at the iron-furnace village of Allaire, married workers resided in row houses only one and one-half stories tall. These structures were of brick, and comprised eleven family units. The fireplace with chimney and stair to the half-floor were on opposite sides of the unit, which included four rooms.

Both Batsto and Allaire villages are now historic sites, undergoing careful preservation and restoration by the State of New Jersey, and are open daily to the visiting public with tour service. Batsto flourished as an iron-furnace village from 1766 to 1848, turning to glassmaking in 1846. Allaire (another iron-furnace hamlet) was in operation from 1813 to 1846.

A typical Batsto village worker's house, built between 1810 and 1820, and the living room of one of the houses. A fire destroyed half the town's houses in 1874, leaving but eighteen structures of this type.

187

The typical Down-Jersey house developed about 1820, and the style continued until the Civil War. Typically, this was a two and one-half story frame building, rectangular, even boxlike in appearance, with a center hall or stair flanked by rooms the depth of the house. Lapped clapboards covered a sturdy braced and pinned framing. Fireplaces and chimneys were at each end of the structure, and completely concealed to the ridge line to reduce heat losses. Among the more notable examples extant is the Morris-Appleyard House in Linwood, built in 1853 by Thomas Morris, deputy collector of customs for the district of Great Egg Harbor, in which the house is located.

During the Civil War era the square boxlike house two stories tall plus a hip roof made its debut, especially along the shore. The hip roof was topped off usually with either an enclosed cupola or exposed "captain's walk." The exposed walks were protected by railings, sometimes of wood, sometimes of iron, cast or wrought.

The Victorian age of gilded architectural opulence affected New Jersey from border to border. Sojourns at the Jersey resorts were all the rage. Steamboats operated regularly from Philadelphia to Cape May, eliminating a rough two-day stagecoach ride. Railroads penetrated the pinelands to the new coast resort of Atlantic City. Having a "cottage at the shore" was the thing to do, if one was

The Nathaniel Holmes House, c. 1822, is an early example of the typical Down-Jersey house. Holmes was a ship chandler of Dennisville and part owner of a number of vessels built in that early Cape May County shipbuilding village. *Home of Mr. and Mrs. Raymond Dixon.*

The Tilton House in Absecon, c. 1840. *Home of Mr. and Mrs. Fred Noyes.*

The Morris-Appleyard House is one of the finest examples of the Down-Jersey house. It was built in Linwood in 1853 by the local customs officer. *Home of Mr. and Mrs. Harold Appleyard.*

to keep abreast of the Joneses, and the construction of frame houses flourished. These cottages were spacious, with high-ceilinged rooms, and large heavy doors and moldings.

Cape May City, situated on the southernmost tip of the state, is a treasure-trove of Victorian architecture. A popular spa since the early nineteenth century, the town has created Victorian Village, Inc., a nonprofit organization that is successfully striving to retain for the resort a prime resource, the wonderful old houses and hotels that give the town character and identity.

Domestic architecture is a living phase of history, and old houses, the largest of our antique treasures, are to be valued, protected, and enjoyed by all who view or live in them.

An unusual example of middle-class Victorian domestic architecture is the wonderful Pink House, c. 1880, located among a treasure-trove of contemporary structures in Cape May City, at the southern tip of the state.

The houses in Fairmount Park

BY ROBERT C. SMITH, *University of Pennsylvania and Winterthur Museum*

IN FAIRMOUNT PARK there are twenty-three houses of architectural distinction built before 1850. Most of them were constructed where they now stand on the banks of the Schuylkill River, but others were moved to the park when threatened with destruction. Together they provide, within a small protected zone, a unique collection representing domestic architecture in the Philadelphia area between about 1700 and 1835.

The park houses can be grouped in three main categories. First, the dwellings in the Delaware River Valley vernacular mode of informal, field-stone construction, with its pent eaves between stories (Letitia Court House, The Monastery), gable façades (Cedar Grove, Ridgeland), and occasional medieval German reminiscences of plan and fenestration (Rittenhouse Cottage). These buildings range in date from 1707 to about 1800.

Next there are the Palladian revival houses of the period from around 1750 to 1780, designed with hip roofs and pedimented façades and doorcases. Characteristically Philadelphian are the narrow proportions of the center pavilions (Laurel Hill, Mount Pleasant, Woodford), and the ample forms and rich detail of the Doric doorways that derive from the State House of Pennsylvania (Independence Hall). Also echoing the State House are the Palladian interior friezes and niches (Woodford, Mount Pleasant) and the stairs with their ramp balustrades and twist newels (Belmont, Laurel Hill, Mount Pleasant).

Finally there are the houses of the Federal period, built between 1780 and 1810, generally with plastered stone walls, and in some cases cubelike plans and elevations (Ormiston, Rockland, The Solitude), similar to those of contemporary though larger houses in coastal New England. These Federal houses of Fairmount Park also have in common the use of rear piazzas for viewing the river, a detail which seems to have been almost as typical of this area as side galleries were of Charleston, South Carolina. Some of the houses of this period offer rooms with curving walls (Chamounix, Lemon Hill), mantels with small-scale classical ornaments of plaster composition (The Lilacs, Ormiston, Strawberry Mansion, Sweetbrier), and the gouged and punched woodwork in simpler geometric designs that is characteristic of the Delaware River Valley (Ridgeland, Strawberry Mansion).

Also in Fairmount Park there is a rare example of early eighteenth-century row-house architecture (Letitia Court House), moved from another site. Arnest is an equally rare reflection of early nineteenth-century English Regency design with notable contemporary woodwork. There are a substantial farmhouse of the 1820's (Greenland) and a house representing the taste of the Greek revival (Hatfield House), brought from North Philadelphia, whose façade furnishes the temple portico indispensable for any truly representative survey of early American architecture, while the Gothic revival stable of Chamounix provides another essential element.

As an aid to the study of the houses of Fairmount Park the following brief directory has been prepared. As noted certain houses are open to the public; others may be visited by special appointment. For appointments and information regarding visiting hours and fees apply to the Philadelphia Museum of Art.

Cedar Grove (see p. 511). The earliest portion of the house, thought to have been constructed in the 1730's, was enlarged in 1752 and doubled in size between 1791 and 1799, when such Federal details as the lunette attic window and some of the interior woodwork were introduced. Architecturally the chief points of interest are the gambrel profile of the gabled entrance façade and the numerous cupboards in the wainscot. The house was moved to its present site from Harrowgate. Open to the public.

Arnest. Thought to have been erected c. 1800-1810, this plastered brick house takes its name from its last owner. Its plan has the English Regency features of tripartite windows and a pair of semi-octagonal bays flanking the front porch. The fine woodwork includes several arched doorways with a rare pseudo-bamboo molding, lotus-flower brackets in the stair, and a handsome reeded mantel in the north bedroom.

Chamounix (Montpelier). Built c. 1800 of brick, this large Federal mansion has a semicircular south bay reminiscent of those of The Woodlands, the contemporary Hamilton mansion in West Philadelphia. This bow is distinguished by an ornamental exterior niche. Chamounix also has an attractive east porch of cast iron and a fine Gothic revival stable of c. 1830-1850.

Glen Fern (Livezey House). A rambling stone house, dramatically set beside the falls of the Wissahickon, acquired by Thomas Livezey in 1747. The principal section belongs to a group of early Philadelphia houses with a central façade balcony. The present one is, however, not original.

Belmont. The main portion of the house, built c. 1755 of brick with stone quoins, lintels, and a door surround, has a central great room with Palladian pedimented doorcases and chimney breast and a unique plaster ceiling of late seventeenth-century English style. A tower (c. 1760), based on that of the State House, contains an important stair with rococo brackets. The third story and piazza are nineteenth-century additions. Open in summer as a restaurant.

The Cliffs. A small mid-eighteenth-century dwelling of plastered stone whose plan and woodwork suggest the fusion of a modest row house with a small mansion. The best feature of the interior, which is wainscoted throughout, is the cross-setted panel of the parlor chimney breast, the simplest version in a series that culminates at Mount Pleasant. The identical north and south façades bear a similar relation to Mount Pleasant.

Greenland. Built about 1825, with central hall flanked by pairs of rooms, this ample farmhouse of plastered stone has retained little of its original woodwork beyond a few interior doors with square panels.

Except as noted, photographs by the author.

Hatfield House. Evolved from a small structure of c. 1760, Hatfield retains very little of the original house. It was modernized about 1835 with the addition of the west end, including the Greek revival portico and south door, sheathing the whole house in flush board siding, rarely used in this area. The ground floor, open to the public, has Greek revival woodwork and marble mantels. Until 1930 Hatfield stood on Hunting Park Avenue at Clarissa Street.

Laurel Hill (Randolph House). The original center section of this brick mansion, built c. 1748-1760, has typical Philadelphia Palladian doorways, chimney breasts, mantels, and stairs. The Federal addition, in larger scale, contains a unique octagonal room and a rare mantel with two tiers of paired reeded colonnettes.

Lemon Hill (The Hills) (see p. 531). A late eighteenth-century house of plastered brick notable for its plan, in which the Federal feature of an oval room is applied in three stories, Lemon Hill also has curving interior and exterior stairs, a hall floor of marble, and an Italian marble mantel of classical design, like those imported for Robert Morris' Philadelphia town house. Open to the public.

Letitia Court House (Letitia Street House). Built in Letitia Court by John Short, carpenter, 1713-1715, and removed to the park in 1883, this Philadelphia row house of brick has a typical eighteenth-century two-room plan, angle fireplace with bolection mantel, characteristic stair, and a rare flat hood with baroque carving over the front doorway, a seventeenth-century English motif found also in New Jersey. Temporarily closed. *Photograph by courtesy of the Philadelphia Museum of Art.*

The Lilacs. Built of partly plastered stone, the house has a mid-eighteenth-century section with corner fireplace and adjacent stair characteristic of Pennsylvania farmhouses. This contrasts with a two-story Federal addition containing Adamesque mantels of about 1795, one with composition heads of Franklin and Washington.

The Monastery (Gorgas House). Built in the 1740's by Joseph Gorgas as a residence for the followers of the mystical Johannes Kelpius, this "monastery" is the finest surviving example of the great stone residences with pent eaves between the stories that appear in the Peter Cooper view of Philadelphia of c. 1720. Characteristic of the Delaware Valley is the concave plastered facing of the pent. With the exception of a kitchen fireplace, the interior was completely altered in the nineteenth century.

Mount Pleasant (Clunie) (see p. 521). Built in 1761, this is architecturally the most important building in Fairmount Park. The plan is unusual because of the separate flanking structures, characteristic of early eighteenth-century Virginia building. The mansion is constructed of plastered rubble walls with brick quoins and belt course and a masonry basement. The interior woodwork includes a Doric frieze (hall), "fish" husks, ornamental niche, an acanthus-carved mantel (parlor), and a rococo chimney breast (upstairs parlor), all closely related to Samuel Harding's wood carving at the State House (1750's). Open to the public.

Ormiston. A Federal brick house of 1798, not unrelated to Rockland. Its best exterior feature is the single pedimented dormer, while the only distinguished interior details are the two fine downstairs mantels enriched with composition eagles and a boy with a dolphin respectively, that approach the elegance of Robert Wellford's style. The front porch is not original.

Ridgeland (Mount Prospect). A stone house of c. 1790-1810, notable for its high gabled façade that suggests the flanks of the great stone barns of Pennsylvania. The proportions and woodwork of the hall are characteristic of Philadelphia, as are the Federal stair and the punched and gouged mantels of the parlor, which may originally have been in another house.

Rittenhouse Cottage. Built by the German immigrant William Rittenhouse in 1707 adjacent to a Wissahickon mill, the small stone structure is set against a hill so as to provide entrances at two levels, like the bank barns brought to Pennsylvania by settlers from the German Palatinate. Characteristic are the gable date stone, casement windows, and steep medieval gable.

Rockland. Erected c. 1800, this is one of the handsomest Federal dwellings in Philadelphia. Especially interesting are the delicate curved front porch similar to that of McIntire's Pingree House in Salem, Massachusetts (1804-1805), and the graceful curved stair in two flights. The plaster ceiling and groove-and-rosette woodwork are typical of the late Federal style in Philadelphia.

The Solitude. Built in 1785 by John Penn, The Solitude has exterior woodwork transitional to the Federal style and an important second-story room with Adamesque plaster ceiling and a doorcase with bound-leaf frieze. These features suggest the Maryland architect Joseph Horatio Anderson, who is believed to have worked in Philadelphia.

Strawberry Mansion (see p. 529). The largest house in Fairmount Park. The central section with its fine Federal dormers, hall with four ornamental niches, and adjacent stair was begun in 1797. North and south wings were added after 1825. Open to the public.

Sweetbrier (see p. 525). Built in 1797, Sweetbrier was one of the first Philadelphia houses to have long first-floor windows. Especially interesting are the muntins of the hall window, the Adamesque treatment of the Palladian arch that divides the hall, and the parlor mantels decorated with plaster composition motifs popular in this area. Open to the public.

Tom Moore Cottage. An eighteenth-century gambrel-roofed story-and-a-half farmhouse of rubble, closely related to the Caleb Pusey House of 1683 in Upland, Pennsylvania, and the Andrew Hendrickson House of 1690 now in Wilmington. Typical of this area are the square façade windows and the corner fireplaces. Picturesquely located on the riverbank, on part of what was the Belmont estate, the house takes its name from the legend that it was occupied by the Irish poet Tom Moore in the summer of 1804. Open to the public.

Woodford (see p. 515). Built c. 1735 and enlarged in 1756, this house along with Mount Pleasant has the finest Palladian exterior woodwork in Fairmount Park. Notable are the cove cornices of the older rooms (hall and parlor) and the pedimented chimney breast of the parlor, whose naturalistically carved swags herald the rococo decoration of Philadelphia Chippendale furniture of the 1760's. The woodwork of the dining room and the great stair are Federal. Open to the public.

Odessa, Delaware

BY AARON G. FRYER

Odessa's Main Street. In foreground, frame and log house (c. 1740) with bay window and cellar doorway; beyond, brick house (c. 1772) with old pump in front. Both houses restored by H. Rodney Sharp. *Photographs by the author.*

Doorway of the colonial brick house (c. 1772). Old pump and well at left.

Twenty-two miles south of Wilmington, Delaware, on U. S. Route 13, lies the crossroads village of Odessa. Although apparently little known beyond the boundaries of its state, Odessa possesses several exceptionally fine examples of colonial architecture and has preserved, or regained through restoration, much of its eighteenth-century character.

Most of the town lies east of the busy highway, stretching back to the Appoquinimink Creek. It is believed that as early as 1659 there was a tiny community here known as Appoquinimie Landing. In 1731 Richard Cantwell built a toll bridge across the river where the modern bridge now stands, and the village became known as Cantwell's Bridge. It was long popular as a stopping place for travelers from the Delaware to the Chesapeake, but in the 1800's assumed greater importance as the principal grain market of the region. Six large granaries stood on the banks of the Appoquinimink, and from 1820 until 1840 some four hundred thousand bushels of grain, brought from a considerable distance, were shipped annually to both domestic and foreign ports. The name was changed from Cantwell's Bridge to Odessa after the great grain port of Russia. But in the 1840's the Delaware Railroad by-passed the town and eventually drew the grain traffic away, leaving Odessa the peaceful hamlet we see today.

Odessa's early prosperity is reflected in many lovely homes. By far the finest is the Corbit house (1772), described in the preceding article. Next to it is the David Wilson house, a splendid example of Georgian architecture built in 1769 for David Wilson, a prosperous merchant who lived in it until his death in 1808. Somewhat similar to the Corbit house in treatment, it is apparently the work of the same builders, Robert May & Company. It is in almost original condition except for the addition of modern conveniences and of a room on the first floor providing more space for the Corbit Library, which since 1924 has been located in the room to the left of the center hall. This was the first free library in Delaware, founded by the will of Dr. James Corbit in 1846 and made operative a year later. The Wilson house was repaired by Mrs. E. Tatnall Warner, a great-granddaughter of the first owner, who acquired it in 1901. The Mary Corbit Warner Museum, containing exotic objects collected by her from all corners of the world, is also housed here. The living room to the right of the center hall and two bedrooms are appropriately furnished in period pieces.

Two other colonial buildings have recently been restored by H. Rodney Sharp, owner of the Corbit house. The brick house, erected about 1772, was once a store, and part of the second floor a lodge room. An old well with wood-encased pump, standing on the brick sidewalk in front, formerly served as the local water supply. In the frame and log house (c. 1740) the logs are of white oak, and the interior has noteworthy woodwork and floors with beaded beams in the kitchen.

Across the street is the old inn, now a private residence. Hand-hewn ship's masts serve as posts of the front porch in the newer portion which was added in 1822 to a pre-Revolutionary two-story brick saltbox. The Lore house, once owned by Chief Justice Charles B. Lore, retains its original end constructed about 1740 of cedar logs, and a curious overhanging attic in the rear.

The Mailly, Thomas, and Whitby houses, and a small dilapidated frame structure known as the Croft house,

The William Corbit, house built 1772, the finest colonial building in Odessa. Restored by its present owner, H. Rodney Sharp.

The Corbit house doorway. Note unusual arrangement of louvers in the blinds.

Old Drawyer's Presbyterian Church, begun in 1773, of brick, with a fine pillared doorway.

Small brick cottage, thought to be the original manse of Old Drawyer's Church. Restored.

The Friends Meeting House, built 1783, is only 20 feet square; well preserved and still in use.

The frame and log house (c. 1740), facing its informal garden.

as well as a cozy brick cottage thought to be the original manse of Old Drawyer's Church, are among the other colonial dwellings in Odessa. Just beyond the Appoquinimink on Lower King's Highway is Fairview, a house built about 1773 for Major James Moore, an original member and treasurer of the Society of the Cincinnati. Most of these have had later alterations, but the Whitby house and Fairview are soon to be restored.

At the west end of town is a small, plain, brick building, the Friends Meeting House, built by David Wilson in 1783. Still in use and in excellent condition, it served as a station in the Underground Railway of slave days.

Old Drawyer's Church is located a short distance beyond the town limits on the Du Pont Highway. It is a substantial-looking structure of brick, built in 1773 to replace a much earlier building. Like the Corbit and Wilson houses, Old Drawyer's is believed to be the work of Robert May & Company. Its beautiful woodcarving is attributed to one Bennet, a partner of Duncan Beard, clockmaker near Odessa in the eighteenth century.

Wilson house doorway, a handsome Georgian example.

The David Wilson house, built 1769, is open free to the public Thursdays and Saturdays.

MEDIEVAL CONSTRUCTION AT EPHRATA

By G. EDWIN BRUMBAUGH

ONE EVENING toward the end of winter, in the year 1732, the little Dunker congregation on the Conestoga had assembled in the rude cabin of a pioneer. They were there at the call of their pastor and teacher, the good Conrad Beissel. Some of them had journeyed miles over chill forest trails, and forded icy streams, to hear this remarkable preacher, whose strong convictions and mystical language convinced them, but seldom brought them peace. In months past, the Brethren in Germantown, aroused by reports of strange doctrines on their frontier of Pennsylvania, had sent their zealous Elders to hear and to exhort. The civil authorities, not interested in doctrines, but zealous in the law, had confined some of their number in prison, because the community persisted in observing the scriptural Sabbath and working upon the legal Sunday. But most distressing of all, certain pious wives left their less "advanced" husbands for a life of spiritual solitude in obedience to their pastor's teaching.

But this night no dissension was in store. Instead they were to witness an unusual scene. After discoursing much on the Kingdom of God, their beloved pastor impressively appointed Elders, handed them the New Testament with the earnest charge to follow its word in governing the congregation, and then laid down his office. Renouncing the strife and worldliness of society, he journeyed eight miles into the wilderness to the crude hut of a kindred spirit, Emanuel Eckerling, who dwelt in holy solitude beside the peaceful waters of the Cocalico. Here Conrad Beissel hoped to await the Second Coming in pious contemplation. Instead, the Ephrata "Settlement of the Solitary" was born. For no sooner had

he cleared his little plot of ground than others followed, and soon the forest was dotted with cabins. This time no Germantown Mother Church could interfere, the civil law was far away, and only the truly "awakened" joined the fervent worship.

Quickly the Settlement grew, and in less than a decade four great timber structures housed the celibate Brotherhood and Sisterhood, and a strong congregation of married "householders," established upon surrounding farms, attended services in "Zion's Saal." Today, although these first large buildings are but a memory, others of equal interest, and almost as old, remain. A strangely medieval Saal, or house of prayer, built for the congregation in 1740; a steep-roofed log convent, the last home of the Sisterhood, and known as Saron; a quaint stone Almonry, where bread was baked for free distribution to the poor; and five cabins scattered in the meadow, still attest a notable past.

When this historic site was acquired by the Commonwealth

FIG. 1 (*right*) — THE FIVE-STORY SOUTH GABLE OF THE EPHRATA SAAL. Partially restored. On the first floor, galvanized iron sheets have been removed; hand-split and shaved clapboards are in place. *Photographs by the author.*

FIG. 2 (*below*) — HALF-TIMBERED FRAME OF SOUTH GABLE, SAAL. Mortised and tenoned oak frame of timbers six inches thick, with stone and clay fill between. Note vertical nailing cleats spaced to receive the original clapboards, which were five Palatine feet in length.

of Pennsylvania in 1939, and the planning of restorations began, the ancient Saal received first attention for many reasons. And the attention was none too soon. As in many another early structure, the honest workmen at Ephrata made some rather bad mistakes in judgment. The foundations had been started upon sharply sloping ledge rock, at some places less than a foot below grade, with no better mortar than simple clay between the stones. Upon this insecure base a great half-timbered frame, mortised and tenoned together in true medieval fashion, with heavy stone and clay fill between the squared oak timbers, was reared five stories to the topmost attic. The walls, twisted and sagging, had spread dangerously as the foundations slipped and settled with the passing years. Timber sills had rotted away, and the decayed ends of posts were supported on precarious wedges of fieldstone. Makeshift sheathing of many sorts, the accumulation of centuries of patching, covered the ancient frame. There were sawed and beveled

carried out. It is necessary here to explain that, three years after the erection of the Saal, a large house of logs, seventy-two feet in length, had been reared, directly adjoining the new "house of prayer." In due time, this building was assigned to the use of the Sisterhood, and named Saron. For reasons related to the involved story of its inception, it had been so placed that it actually overlapped the Saal for a distance of some five feet. Where the two walls lay against one another, narrow doors had been cut through on both first and second floors to allow passage from one building to the other. In the course of the delicate shoring operations, it seemed advisable to place a building jack in the first floor doorway, and the broad board lining of the opening was carefully removed, with most unexpected results. The two buildings had not been built tightly against one another, as had always been supposed, because the projecting structural timbers of the Saal compelled the builders to leave a space about six inches wide between them. In this space, sealed from view for two centuries, the original outside clapboards of the Saal were still in place.

With these unquestionably original clapboards before us, a real task unfolded: their duplication. The originals were five feet, two inches long (which, according to the old Palatine scale, was just five feet), about seven inches wide, a scant half-inch thick along one side, and knife-edged along the other. They had obviously been split and shaved from great red oak logs. Research and inquiry revealed some information as to early methods of clapboard making, and resulted in the acquisition of an antique "frow" for splitting logs, a gift of the Landis Valley Museum near Lancaster. This all-important tool consists of a heavy blade, slightly less than a foot in length, with the metal at one end curled around to form an "eye," in which is inserted a stubby wooden handle at right angles

FIG. 3 — NEEDLE SHOR-ING UNDER SOUTH GABLE OF SAAL. The original stone and clay fill may still be seen between the timbers of the frame.

FIG. 4 (below) — SLOP-ING LEDGE ROCK UN-DER SAAL WALLS. On this sloping ledge, the original foundations were built.

FIG. 5 (below) — RECONSTRUCTED CORNER OF SAAL. New stone foundations started on level base chiseled out of solid rock. Old timber frame repaired wherever rotted.

boards, hand-split lath and plaster, various kinds of clapboards, and even simulated brickwork, made of galvanized iron sheets. Obviously, one of the first problems was to determine the original outside finish of the half-timbered frame. There was even the possibility that the timbers had been exposed. After careful study of historical documents and of evidence at the building, a conclusion was reached, which was confirmed beyond possibility of dispute in a most interesting way.

In order to repair the walls and

replace the spreading foundations, it was necessary to "needle-shore" the building. By this is meant the insertion through the outer walls, at regular intervals, of heavy timbers called "needles." These needles were then raised slowly with heavy building jacks until dangerous sagging was corrected, and then supported temporarily on oak posts. One section of the outer wall at a time, with all its super-structure, was thus held suspended in the air while reconstruction was to the back of the blade. After the logs are split into quarters, the frow is placed, blade down, on one end of a quarter section, and driven into the wood by striking the free end opposite the handle with a frow club, very much like a short, thick, baseball bat. Our first laborious attempts, the conflicting but welcome advice of authorities, and our own "improvements" upon the devices used, which led to near frustration, comprise a story by itself.

Finally, a deliberate search was instituted to locate some old craftsman whose early experience, or memory of still earlier traditions, could supply us with the forgotten cunning needed for our task. The search was strikingly successful. Back in the Furnace Mountains of Lancaster County we discovered an elderly sawmill owner, with the necessary knowledge, who taught us how to make and use a "splitting rock," capable of controlling the direction of the split. This simple but forgotten piece of equipment, or something very similar, must have been used by the Brothers of Ephrata, although none of the authorities consulted mentioned such a device. Now we are producing clapboards with reasonable economy and speed. They are finished with a large draw knife on a "schnitzelbank" or shaving horse, made from measurements of an early original in the museum of our friends at Landis Valley.

Curiously enough, an excellent description of the type of construction used in the venerable old Saal is contained in an account by Jasper Dankers and Peter Sluyter of a visit to the settlements of northern Jersey in 1679 and 1680. "Most of the English," they wrote, "and many others, have their houses made of nothing but clap-boards, as they call them, in this manner: they first make a wooden frame, the same as they do in Westphalia, and at Altona, but not so strong; they then split the boards of clapwood, so that they are like cooper's pipe staves, except they are not bent. These are made very thin, so that the thickest end is about a little finger thick, and the other is made sharp like the edge of a knife. They are about five or six feet long, and are nailed on the outside of the frame, with the ends lapped over each other. They are not usually laid so close together as to prevent you from sticking a finger between them, in consequence of either not being well jointed, or the boards being crooked. When it is cold and windy the best people plaster them with clay." Down to the last detail this description applies to the Saal, even

Fig. 6 (*right*) — Unrestored West Doorway of Saal. This photograph, taken fifteen years ago, shows the appearance of the doorway during the past century.

Fig. 7 (*below*) — Restored West Doorway of Saal. As it appeared when first constructed. Arched head of door discovered under plaster. A new square-headed, narrow door had been inserted inside the original opening.

to the stronger frame than those observed by Dankers and Sluyter, thus indicating Continental origin. Without doubt it is one of the most remarkable early buildings in America. In spite of its frontier crudity and deliberate ascetic plainness, it speaks with the language of old-world medievalism. It has always attracted the curious, and remains one of Pennsylvania's most prized relics of the past

In all of the restoration work at Ephrata, the same materials and the same methods originally employed are being used, so far as practical. Only damaged or repaired parts of buildings will be disturbed, unless reconstruction is necessary for safety. In general, only rotted sections of posts and timbers are being cut out. Sound pieces of seasoned wood are then bolted in place, instead of replacing the entire timber. All sections so added are carefully marked for easy identification even a century hence, and the determination of every detail is the result of the most painstaking research and study. The task is slow and discouraging to anyone looking for speedy and impressive results. In fact, there is little to indicate the very real progress made to date toward the ultimate restoration. But the Saal is now structurally safe and almost all of its many puzzling riddles have been solved. The west front, with its newly discovered arched doorway, is completely restored. And, although operations today are limited to essential repairs, these are being made properly and in line with the final program. The buildings are constantly watched and protected day and night, while the course is being charted for complete restoration in happier days to come.

Eventually, the entire State-owned portion of the original "Kloster" property will be restored in a scholarly manner.

The architecture of Salem

BY WILLIAM J. MURTAGH, *Director, department of education, National Trust for Historic Preservation*

THE EARLIEST MAP to show the plan adopted for the settlement of Salem is dated April 2, 1766, and is attributed to Frederick William Marshall, the then *oeconomus* (administrator) of Wachovia. An exchange of letters between Brother Johann Ettwein and Brother Marshall in 1765 gives us evidence of the Moravians' concern for the appearance of their city: "Regarding the plan of the town, we in the Conference are agreed how it should be . . . Regarding the Square, we all thought it too long; because none but two-story houses will be built on the Square; the place in the middle is made to appear so much larger than if three- or four-story houses were built around it. Besides, if it were shorter it would be more even and level."

The actual construction of the community began on January 6, 1766: "Monday, a dozen Brethren partly from Bethania, partly from Bethabara, took a wagon and went to the new town site where in the afternoon they cut down the trees on the place where the first house was to stand, singing as they worked . . ." The original plan gave prominence to the rectangular central square, with streets perpendicular to each other in the vicinity of the square creating a gridiron.

Foundation stone for the first house was laid on the main street on June 6 of that year. Stone that could be conveniently broken to proper size was used and the pieces were laid in clay because there was a scarcity of lime for mortar. At Marshall's suggestion half-timber construction was recommended for the superstructure chiefly because of the lack of a sawmill and the expense of hauling wood from Bethabara approximately six miles away. The spaces between the heavy timbers were filled with brick or laths wrapped in a mixture of straw and clay to form cylinders of proper size, which were then slipped into the grooved sides of the framing and pressed down to create a solid wall the thickness of the frame.

Fig. 1. The outstanding monument of the once busy center of Bethabara is the Church, consecrated in November 1788 at a time when Salem already completely overshadowed its earlier neighbor. The stone walls of the structure, pargeted and marked off in an ashlar design, are pierced by a series of fully arched windows and doors along what is now the highway façade, and on the gable end two arched windows with a small arched window above. A well-proportioned octagonal bell tower with concave conical roof is topped by a weather vane. A slightly smaller gable-roofed section has characteristic red brick segmental arches over the windows.

2. The 1784 Tavern is important because it helped to set the architectural
...acter of the community; it occupies the same site as an earlier half-timbered
...rn which burned. The utilitarian placing of the windows on the gable end is
...esting, as is the lack of windows opening onto the porch. Typical flat or seg-
...ed arches and the usual 11½-inch brick set in Flemish bond are illustrated here.
...depth of the plate at the roof line is a Germanic feature.

3. The Salem Community Store is typical of the early efforts to conserve scarce
... The building, erected in 1775, is of field stone laid in clay to the gable, with
...in coat of lime plaster marked into an ashlar finish. The one-piece shutters, a
...itarian idea, were used in the earliest days of Salem. The building shows the
...cal roof kick at the eave line over a diagonal board cornice. Instead of the more
...l handmade clay tiles the roof was covered with shingles.

Such Dutch "biscuits" are comparable to brick
nogging but leave something to be desired as far
as durability is concerned, although a subsequent
coating of lime plaster or the application of clapboards can solve the erosion problem. It appears
that bricks were made in Salem as early as the
latter part of 1766, although brick was not used
for complete construction until the building of
the second tavern twenty years later (Fig. 2).
However, brick does seem to have been used as
filling in earlier structures of half-timber construction.

This latter method was utilized in the earliest
major building still standing in the community,
the Single Brothers' House of 1768-1769 (color
plate and Fig. 15). In half-timber construction
(essentially medieval, though it continued in
Germany until the twentieth century) the upright
timbers of the framing were spaced two to three
feet apart with diagonal bracing placed where
needed. The interstices were then filled with
brick nogging, pargeted and whitewashed on
the inside. The façade facing the square was developed with a system of three six-over-six-light
windows evenly spaced across the two floors, and
an overlighted entrance door. An amply proportioned gable roof with the characteristic kick, or
spring, at the eave line covered the upper and
lower attic portions. Because of the nature of the
construction, a pent eave girdled the structure
between the first and second floors.

Inside, the building has many of the same
architectural characteristics as some of the early
buildings in Bethlehem, including the Single
Brothers' House in that city: smooth whitewashed
walls, handmade pavers, and wide plank floors.

In 1786, a fifty-three-foot addition was made
to the structure on the downhill side. Eleven-and-
a-half-inch brick laid up in Flemish bond and
flat- or segmented-arch windows carried on the
building tradition established in the earlier settlements. In the restoration of this building, its
architectural potential, especially that of the older
portion, has been realized to make it one of the
most startling structures in America today—a seg-
ment of medieval Germanic Europe transferred
to the Western Hemisphere.

Although small buildings undoubtedly continued to be erected in the community, the next
major structure was the *Gemein Haus* built opposite the Brothers' House on the square in 1771
and consecrated in November of that year. The
structure was destroyed in 1854, but it is known
from documentary sources to have been a large
two-story building, with pent eaves like those on
the restored Brothers' House separating the stone
first story from the half-timbered second, with
gable roof covering an upper and lower attic,
and presumably with the characteristic kick at the
eave line. According to Dr. Adelaide Fries, historian of the southern Moravians, the structure
was "improved" during the later years of the
eighteenth century when the pent was removed
and the surfaces were plastered and marked off in
white in an ashlar design to simulate cut stone.

Fig. 4. Matthew Miksch's small house and shop of logs covered with clapboards (1771). Note the protrusion of the plates at the roof corners and the unusual height from the windows to the eaves. The house and the tobacco manufactory in the rear have old Germanic tile roofs; the thumb-mold print on each tile guides water to the center of the tile below it, allowing the tiles to be laid with the joints aligned, instead of alternating. The entrance door in herringbone pattern with three-pane overlight and shingled gable above it is characteristic, as is the red-tile roof with gentle kick at the eaves and the central chimney. In its three-room plan this house is representative of the earliest type in Salem.

The Anna Catherina House, a small clapboard structure in the garden behind the John Vogler House (Figs. 10, 11) is somewhat less foreign in architectural character than the Miksch House (Fig. 4), although it is similar in its smallness of scale and in its use of clapboarding. Both have the same three-room floor plan.

A house for the Single Sisters was erected in 1786 at the southeast corner of the square. The brickwork contrasts dark headers with salmon-color stretchers, giving the building a look of great quality. It is notable for its original Germanic tile roof. The double tier of dormers is an addition of 1811. Many of the characteristics already noted in other structures in the community, such as the flat arches over each of the windows and the upper and lower attics under the gable roof, can be observed here. The interior retains the original wide pine floors, hardware, and characteristic plank-balustraded stair run.

The Lick-Boner House (Fig. 5) was erected on a "back street" in 1787. In 1795, Johannes Leinbach, a shoemaker, bought it from Martin Lick. He rebuilt the central chimney, divided the hall

Fig. 5. The Lick-Boner House, 1787. Interesting architectural details here are the sill and roof plates which extend beyond the main wall and are finished with chamfered edges ending in a "lamb's tongue." The 1795 lean-to addition, which is nogged with clay and straw, has rather unusual matched bevel-edged boarding. It is notable for its finished quality.

from the kitchen, and added the lean-to-shop. In the process of restoration the removal of weatherboarding exposed the original log construction. Though an architectural throwback to an earlier tradition, this little structure has all the Continental features associated with the earliest buildings the Moravians erected in their community, such as the single unshuttered six-over-six-light window and herringbone-pattern "Dutch" door with overlight, both relatively small voids in the

solid expanse of the façade, and the massive central brick chimney.

The 1790's saw development of the north side of the square with the erection in 1794 of the Boy's School building at the west end and the *Vorsteher's* House of 1797 north of it. The school building has the architectural attributes one associates with late eighteenth-century Moravian building in Salem, for example the foundation of rubble stone, plastered and marked off in ashlar-style block, which stands a full story high on the street side and is topped by a one-story brick Flemish-bonded structure with diamond pattern worked by dark headers into the west gable (Fig. 6). The even rhythm of solids and voids, each with characteristic flat-arch opening, across the surface of the main façade the single-leaf solid shutters on the first floor and the overlight over the central entrance, not to mention the Germanic tile roof and cove cornice, admirably illustrate this. Its builder was Johann Gottlob Krause, potter and brickmaker to the community. The prime architectural feature of the interior is the plank-balustraded central stair (Fig. 7), which mounts from the first or cellar floor to the second story, which was given over to classroom use, and on to a room under the roof used as a *Schlaf Saal,* or sleeping hall.

The *Vorsteher's* House is forty-two feet long, on a stone foundation eighteen inches thick, with a center hall flanked by two rooms on each side. Two of these are vaulted, one with a corner fire-

Fig. 6. Salem's *Anstalt,* or Boys' School, was built by the potter-builder Johann Gottlob Krause in 1794. The diapered effect of the brick, achieved with dark headers, was a typical Krause decoration. The building retains its original tile roof.

Fig. 7. Boys' School plank-balustraded stair. Johannes Krause's shop was paid £14 for this.

Fig. 8. Hooded roofs over entrance stoops seem to be unique to Salem; the earliest example is on the Church of 1800. Ornamental railings were also featured. This is the entrance to the Inspector's House of 1811.

Fig. 9. Salem houses frequently had two street entrances. The Christoph Vogler House (1797) was equipped with one for the family and another (*right*) for the gunsmith's shop. The forge room could be reached by the steps at the gable end. Note the method employed here, as on the Miksch House, of laying the clay tile roof without staggered joints; thin wooden shakes under the joints helped make it weathertight. All of the architectural characteristics noted in earlier buildings are present here, but indications of an Anglicizing influence are reflected in the intricate molding of the arched overlight of the entrances, which creates an interesting stylistic dichotomy in this charming little building.

Fig. 10. The John Vogler House, 1819. This was the first house in Salem to break with Moravian utilitarian ideas and to present a balanced façade to the street. General proportion, size of windows, regularity of voids, placement of chimneys at gable ends, and much of the detail indicate that the Germanic tradition of the eighteenth century has been superseded: even the element of arched window heads has disappeared.

Fig. 11. This rear view of the John Vogler House shows the 14-by-12-foot rear wing mentioned in Vogler's application for permission to build, which was to serve as the laundry and smithy; a bake oven forms a further appendage. The half-roof form is unique in Salem.

Fig. 12. Brass knob and escutcheon on the house of the silversmith John Vogler, thought to have been made by him.

Fig. 13. By 1828, when Adam Butner planned his "two-storied frame house," Salem architecture had completely broken with early tradition. It was directed that "the porch on the front side of the house, resting on columns, must not in any way damage or hamper the foot path . . . and the stairs must not be wider than three feet." The restored house duplicates the original yellow, green, and red paint colors.

Fig. 14. Window catches of this type are apparently unique to Salem; they are found in buildings dating from 1784 through 1786. The ball counterweight forced the catch into a notch of the window stop as the window was raised.

place on an outside wall. Such fireplaces seem to be an indication of a lessening of Germanic purity, architecturally speaking, since they occur in later eighteenth-century buildings in Salem but not in earlier buildings there or in any of the Pennsylvania settlements. The *Vorsteher's* House of 1797 reflects the typical Moravian structure of the turn of the century in the excellent molded water table, the very pronounced kick of the roof as it approaches the plate, and a finely proportioned cove cornice. The structure also gives evidence of patterning in dark headers on the gable ends.

The bakery that Johann Gottlob Krause designed and erected in 1800 near the *Vorsteher's* House harks back to an earlier esthetic in proportion, scale, and relationship of solids to voids in its street façade; but with the opening years of the nineteenth century, as in the post-Revolutionary years in Bethlehem, the Anglicizing influence in Salem seems to increase progressively. An exception can be noted in the Home Moravian Church, begun in 1797 after the plans of Frederick William Marshall. This was the largest church built in the North Carolina Piedmont at

that time, and its cupola (see cover) offers interesting architectural analogies to that on the Bell House in Bethlehem. The interior of the Church has unfortunately been seriously altered on two occasions but the building still retains much of its original exterior appearance if one can discount the later stained-glass windows.

Such structures as the houses erected for Samuel Benjamin Vierling in 1802 and John Vogler in 1819 (Figs. 10, 11) illustrate well a progression away from the Germanic purity of earlier structures in the community. The Vierling House still uses flat segmental arches over each of the windows, but throughout Salem the great central chimney has been replaced by smaller chimneys at the gable ends of the roof, indicating the use of additional open fireplaces; and the bowed arch with flamboyant mullions recalls the overlights of the Christoph Vogler House (Fig. 9) erected a few years previously. Although exceptions to this trend can be noted in the community, the force of the Germanic tradition is gone—but not before it had left a legacy of unusual structures which make an important contribution to the diversity of America's cultural background.

The Single Brothers' House in Salem was erected in two stages, the half-timbered portion in 1769 and the brick addition in 1786. Half-timbered buildings were nogged with clay and straw reinforced with laths set between the timbers, or with brick of special dimensions, as here. Only two days were required to erect the timbering for the earlier portion of this building.

Fig. 15. Rear view of the 1769 Single Brothers' House. The foundation of the 1786 brick addition (*right*) is plastered and painted in an ashlar pattern.

Fig. 16. Latch and keyhole escutcheon in the Single Brothers' House, 1769.

Fig. 17. Detail of back door of the 1786 addition to the Single Brothers' House, showing double hinging of door to permit wider opening when provisions were brought into the kitchen.

I. The Single Brothers' House.

II.   Miksch House, bedroom.

III.   Salem Tavern, the keeper's quarters.

IV. John Vogler House, dining room.

Seven great

The Colonel William Rhett House. The handsome
dwelling Rhett built for himself c. 1712
is the earliest surviving house in Charleston.
Photograph by Samuel Chamberlain.

The drawing room of the Rhett House represents a successful merging of English and French eighteenth-century furnishings. The Aubusson rugs have an unusual dove-color
background. Against the wall is an English sofa of Sheraton design, flanked by two Louis XV chairs. The other
sofa is French, also Louis XV, with two fine Adam chairs
on either side. The portrait at the far end of the room is by
Coningsby-Smith. Above the English sofa, on either side
of the large portrait of the 1830's, are two silk embroideries,
c. 1800, and, above these, two Italian water colors of Virgil
making his will. *Except as noted, photographs are by Helga
Photo Studio.*

CHARLESTON'S REPUTATION as a city of unusual architectural distinction has never rested on the possession of only a
few fine dwellings, churches, and public buildings but rather
on entire groupings of buildings that form a highly individual
townscape. Within these heavy concentrations of buildings,
however, will be found a number of houses of great importance, equal in finish and design to the finest in America of
comparable periods.

The Colonel William Rhett House

Something of a lone survivor from an earlier period is the
Colonel William Rhett House at 54 Hasell Street, a handsomely restored dwelling that is believed to be the oldest
structure in the city. The Rhetts purchased the property in
1711 and changed its name from the Point Plantation to
Rhettsbury. A 1739 plat of the plantation (it measured
about thirty acres and was fifty yards from the town line)
shows an avenue reaching from King Street, then known as
the High Way, to the house and then extending east to the
Cooper River. On this plan the property is divided to form
a large garden and park rather than what we might think of
as a working country unit. It was probably not long after
1712 that Colonel Rhett built the house that now stands on

Charleston houses

BY W. H. JOHNSON THOMAS

The sitting room on the entrance level of the Daniel Huger House has an unusual marble fireplace surround which appears to be of French origin. On the overmantel panel hangs a fine eighteenth-century water color attributed to François Keizerman, showing an Italian rustic scene. The miniatures on the mantel are of members of the Huger and Izard families. On the south wall are two mid-nineteenth-century *gouaches* of the harbor of Naples. The early nineteenth-century sofa and chairs have been in the Huger family for several generations.

In the dining room of the Huger House, unpaneled except for the dado, as is typical of the north side of Charleston double houses, are a number of late eighteenth - century Charleston - made pieces, including the set of eight chairs and the sideboard. The table was purchased by the Hugers in Virginia at the start of this century. Over the mantel hangs a portrait of Stephen Richard Proctor, attributed to Samuel F. B. Morse (1791-1872). The other two portraits are of Daniel Huger Jr. (left) and Daniel Huger.

The Colonel William Rhett House

The unusual plasterwork on the walls of the dining room
—the only remaining example in Charleston—dates from
c. 1750, the earliest period of stucco decoration in America.
All of the furniture in the room is English; the chairs are
Sheraton. On the table are four matching candlesticks of
Adam design (c. 1770) and an English tankard dated 1711.
The English Chippendale mirror is one of a pair. Over the
mantel is a self-portrait by Christian Seybold (1697-1768),
court painter to Maria Theresa, wife of Holy Roman Emperor Francis I.

The spacious second-story drawing room is noted for its handsome cornice and ornamental plasterwork ceiling, which includes trophies composed of musical instruments. The room contains many family pieces, among which are miniatures of the Horry family by Charles Fraser (1782-1860), a pair of Chippendale mirrors, and a pair of inlaid tables from the Laurens household.

Hasell Street. Constructed on a high basement, the two-story dwelling was made with two rooms across the west side (with what was possibly the main entrance leading into the drawing room) and two small rooms and an entrance hallway with staircase on the east.

There is evidence of several important changes in the house; perhaps the earliest was the addition of unusual plaster wall panels and ornaments in a subdued version of rococo in what is now the dining room. Following a treatment similar to that found in Irish houses of the period, the plasterwork was probably added by Rhett's widow about 1745 or by his granddaughter, Sarah Wright Hasell, not long after 1750. Much of the existing interior today would appear to date from a very complete redecoration about 1800. Possibly at this time the northwest room of the house was extended eleven feet, three inches to the north; the west and east piazzas with their slender columns were added; and the wooden mantels and trim in several rooms installed.

The house remained in the Rhett family until 1807 when it was purchased by Christopher FitzSimons, a wealthy wharf owner. The fortunes of the Rhett House had declined considerably by the early decades of the present century. Shortly before World War II it attracted the attention of Mr. and Mrs. Benjamin Kittredge Jr. They bought the house and its Greek revival neighbor just to the west, making an unusually handsome unit with connecting gardens. They also restored the interior, but few features of the house were altered. The Rhett House is now the home of Mr. and Mrs. Bushrod B. Howard.

The Miles Brewton House was built for a wealthy Charleston merchant c. 1769. Its elaborate carving is the work of Ezra Waite, a carver and builder from London. The house and its extensive dependencies are virtually unchanged from the time of construction and have never left the ownership of the family of Miles Brewton. *Chamberlain photograph.*

The table in the Brewton House dining room was brought from one of the family plantations before the turn of the century. On the table are silver candelabra and a tureen from the Ravenel family. The chandelier of bronze and Waterford glass was brought from a family plantation at Waccamaw Neck c. 1791. In the panel over the mantel is a painting of the *Mackinaw* (c. 1840), a ship owned by John Ravenel who had a fleet of vessels sailing to Russia, Europe, and the Orient. On the mantel are pieces of Manigault armorial China Trade porcelain and English silver candlesticks that belonged to Miles Brewton. The chest-on-chest is attributed to Thomas Elfe.

The Daniel Huger House

As the prosperity of the city grew, the size and elaboration of the more important residences increased. Among the earliest of the surviving houses of size, constructed during what became a major period of local architectural accomplishment, is the Daniel Huger House at 34 Meeting Street. It was built about 1760 by Captain John Bull, Mary Bull, or their granddaughter, Mrs. Daniel Blake.

This three-story structure, raised on a high basement, is an example of the Charleston double house, with a plan of four rooms to a floor, split by a center hallway. Not the city's earliest dwelling of such a plan, it shows an advance in finish and refinement of detail over its older neighbors. It is constructed of English-size, sandy-clay, Low Country brick but is now covered by stucco, perhaps added after the earthquake of 1886 when many local brick buildings were so treated.

Its interior reflects the advances made in what had been a wilderness settlement not many decades earlier, with rooms of generous proportions and fine paneling throughout. On the second story is the broad drawing room, which has handsome plasterwork decoration on the ceiling and a carved overmantel with Ionic pilasters.

At the start of the American Revolution, the house, then owned by Mrs. Blake, was occupied by Lord William Campbell, fourth son of the fourth duke of Argyll, who had only recently come to Charleston as a governor of the Province of South Carolina and had married Sarah Izard, a cousin of Mrs. Blake. Mrs. Blake sold the house to a member of the well-known Morris family of New York in 1795, who in turn sold it to his nephew-in-law, Daniel Elliott Huger, in 1818. The Hugers have retained the property since that date and today it is the residence of Mr. and Mrs. Daniel E. Huger.

The Miles Brewton House

The Miles Brewton House at 27 King Street, built shortly after the Huger House c. 1769, has been called the supreme example of the double house in the city and one of the finest town dwellings in the United States. It was constructed for a distinguished and wealthy Charlestonian, and its carving was done by Ezra Waite, an experienced carver and housebuilder from London.

The two-story dwelling sits on a high basement and is given an added beauty by its two-tier portico—Ionic columns of wood above Doric of Portland stone—with an enriched entablature and pediment. Its rooms are paneled and carved with unparalleled delicacy. The hallway on the entrance level is flagged in red stone and the stairs, which are in a pedimented projection with a large Palladian window, are of mahogany.

The second-story drawing room, which occupies most of the front of the building, attests to the great skill of its carver. Its enrichments are in the Corinthian order, with a scroll-pediment overmantel and a high-cove ceiling painted blue.

As the finest dwelling in Charleston, the Miles Brewton House has been popular with the commanders of invading armies. The British military leaders Sir Henry Clinton and Lords Rawdon and Cornwallis lived here during the Revolution. The Union commanders General Meade and General Hatch occupied the house in 1864 and 1865.

In both its interior details and its furnishings, which include many pieces of English and Charleston-made furniture, the house is still of the period in which it was completed two hundred years ago. Although it has been the home of Brewtons, Mottes, Alstons, Pringles, and Frosts, and is now the residence of Mr. and Mrs. Edward Manigault, it has never passed out of the hands of descendants of Miles Brewton.

In the great drawing room on the second floor of the Brewton House hangs the original chandelier, which has escaped injury for more than two hundred years in spite of an earthquake. Of Anglo-Irish glass, it was designed for this room while the house was being built. The fireplace surround and overmantel are superb examples of Ezra Waite's carving skill.

561

Above the Georgian mantel in the large second-story drawing room is mahogany fretwork trim thought to be by Thomas Elfe, and the two straight chairs in the foreground are attributed to him. The wing chair and the yellow armchair were made in Charleston. An English Chippendale mirror hangs above a particularly fine marble-topped table (c. 1750-1770) which was among the original furnishings of Drayton Hall (see p. 576).

The Heyward-Washington House

The Heyward-Washington House, owned by the Charleston Museum since 1929 and open daily to visitors, was built on its Church Street site about 1770 by Daniel Heyward of a great planter family. He left it to his son, Thomas Heyward, a Signer. During President Washington's visit to Charleston in 1791 the city rented the house from the Heywards for him and his suite. The President noted in his diary that the "lodgings provided for me in this place were very good, being the furnished house of a Gentleman at present in the Country." Since then the house has carried his name.

It is a typical example of the Charleston double house, though more like the Huger House than the Brewton in proportions. The same plan of four rooms to a floor, a central hall, and the large second-story drawing room (extending across the width of what would be the upstairs hallway) provides for pleasant formal living and for adequate circulation of cool breezes in summer. Each room has exposures on two sides and the center hall creates the needed draft. All the rooms are decorated with molded plasterwork and paneling, but only the large second-floor drawing room is paneled from floor to ceiling.

Although it suffered a period of neglect after it passed from the Heyward family, the house has been carefully restored and is now filled with fine Charleston furniture. The deep garden behind the house, which had become completely overgrown, has also been restored as an eighteenth-century garden, planted only with flowers that grew in Charleston when Thomas Heyward lived here and when Washington was a guest.

The Heyward-Washington House was built c. 1770 for Daniel Heyward, a rice planter of St. Luke's Parish. Following the Civil War, the house went through a period of deterioration and much of the first-story front was replaced by display windows. The building was threatened with destruction during the 1920's, but local preservationists were able to purchase it. It has been meticulously restored. Now the property of the Charleston Museum, it is open daily to the public.

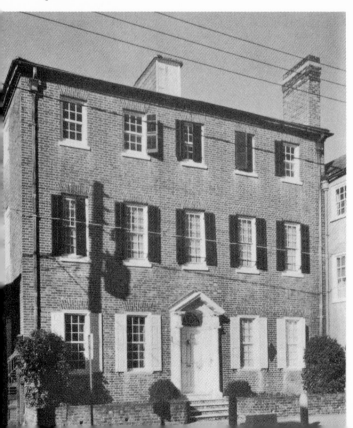

The William Gibbes House

The William Gibbes House, at 64 South Battery, was built after 1772 by a shipowner and merchant. At the time it was the most westerly house on that point of land and faced the Ashley River, with Gibbes' "bridge," or wharf, running out from the house to the water so that from the windows the owner could watch his business activities. In the summer months Gibbes' wharf became a place of recreation for polite society.

The Gibbes House has elements of Palladian design. It is raised a full story above street level, on a rusticated basement, and is crowned by a wide pediment supported by console brackets and accented by a circular window in the center.

The interior reflects the changing fashions of three distinct periods—Georgian, Adam, and post-World War I. When Gibbes died at the end of the Revolution, his house passed to Sarah Moore Smith, whose family was to live here for four generations. The Smiths redecorated quite thoroughly in the Adam style that reached Charleston about 1800. At this time the monumental front stairway was added. Most impressive of the Adam additions is the large second-story ballroom, now used as a drawing room. Its high-cove ceiling is ornamented in the light and graceful Adam manner, with motifs in relief radiating from the cornice and tipped in gilt.

During the nineteenth century the Gibbes House was owned by the Grimke family, and passed to the Reverend John Grimke Drayton, who took his mother's surname in order to inherit Magnolia, the Ashley River plantation. Mrs. Washington A. Roebling, widow of the builder of the Brooklyn Bridge, bought the property in the 1930's, and made extensive additions and improvements to the house and laid out the large gardens behind it. It is now the home of Mrs. Roebling's grandson, John Ashby Farrow, and his wife.

The Joseph Manigault House

The Joseph Manigault House, at 350 Meeting Street, was built between about 1790 and 1803 for a rice planter after designs by his brother, Gabriel Manigault, one of Charleston's earliest native-born architects. It was probably in this three-story dwelling that the Adam style first appeared in South Carolina. Gabriel Manigault had read law at Lincoln's Inn in London for several years beginning in 1777, and brought back to Charleston a modified, almost understated, version of the Adam style that was to dominate the city for twenty-five years.

Joseph Manigault's dwelling was designed more as a country villa than as a town house that had to be fitted on a typically narrow Charleston building lot. This section of Wraggborough, an early nineteenth-century suburb, was still open country at the time and tradition has it that a broad avenue of oaks led from the north entrance of the house down to the Cooper River on the east. For his design Manigault chose a parallelogram, relieved in severity by gentle bays and semicircular piazzas. His floor plan is characterized by an easy intercommunication of service areas and rooms, and each room has colors and plasterwork of the delicacy and airy grace that characterized the Adam style.

Partly because of its remoteness from the center of the city, the Manigault House found itself in trouble early in the twentieth century. It survived use as a boardinghouse and the sale of portions of its lot, but by 1920 the building itself was in danger of demolition. Preservationists came to its aid, but were forced to sell off part of the garden in order to gain funds for restoration. In 1933 an anonymous donor bought the house and gave it to the Charleston Museum. Two years later the part of the garden sold was also given, and the rear garden was restored after measured drawings. Gifts to furnish the house were received and now it holds a fine collection of Louis XV and Louis XVI pieces, Waterford glass, and English porcelains.

The Nathaniel Russell House

Another great Adam house, also once endangered but since 1955 the handsome home of Historic Charleston Foundation, is the imposing Nathaniel Russell House at 51 Meeting Street. Built before 1809 for an elderly Charleston merchant who had come south from his native Rhode Island, it serves not only as a monument to Russell's career but as a last expression of the high period of prosperity during which many of the city's valuable buildings were constructed. The house is designed on the plan of a single house but with a side stair hall, oval rooms, and projecting bays. It has been furnished through contributions with pieces from Charleston and many other parts of the world. The main rooms are a museum and are open daily to the public. It is appropriate that a house of such elegance and historic importance should serve as headquarters for the preservation group that has saved so much of the city from destruction.

Built after 1772 for a wealthy merchant and shipowner at the height of Charleston's Georgian period, the William Gibbes House has been extensively renovated twice and today handsomely combines several periods. *Chamberlain photograph.*

The pictorial wallpaper in the long central hall at the entrance level of the Gibbes House is a reproduction of *Eldorado* designed by Ehrmann and Zipelius in 1848 and printed by Jean Zuber. On the left is a delicate Empire sofa with brass mounts. Facing it is an English hunt board which shows strong Adam influence. The long rug in the foreground is a Kermanshah.

Above the mantel of the upstairs drawing room hangs the fine portrait of Mrs. Peter Manigault painted by Jeremiah Theus in 1757. The Sèvres porcelain urns on the mantel are set with Wedgwood jasperware plaques. The scroll-back chairs and sofa, thought to be American, are from the Pinckney family, c. 1815. The tea tables were made in Charleston and the silver service is from Philadelphia.

The Joseph Manigault House, completed c. 1803 for a wealthy rice planter, is probably the earliest example of the Adam style in South Carolina. At the turn of the century the house had declined in fortune and was in danger of being destroyed, but efforts of local preservationists resulted in its restoration. It belongs now to the Charleston Museum and is open daily to the public. *Chamberlain photograph.*

The deep central hall on the ground floor of the Manigault House extends to a circular staircase in a projecting north bay. The two standing candelabra were possessions of the Simons family. The three chairs were made in Charleston c. 1815.

The long dining room of the Manigault House ends in a bay on the east. The handsome gray-green walls and the delicate plaster decorations below the cornice are typical of the Adam style. The Sheraton dining table and the set of late classic chairs are American. Inset on the stay rails of the chairs are silver plaques engraved with the crest of the Mathews family. John Mathews was elected governor of South Carolina in 1782. The American sideboard is believed to have been made in Charleston, and American silver is displayed on it. The tilt-top tables in front of the windows are also locally made. The porcelain coffee service on the dining table is French.

The Nathaniel Russell House was built before 1809 by a successful merchant prince who had moved from Bristol, Rhode Island, to this southern seaport. While its plan and style are unusual for Charleston, the house is one of a splendid group built in the early 1800's; the brickwork, window arches, and keystones, and the use of a red brick in the trim find several handsome counterparts in the city. Inside, too, the house has some typical Charleston features and some details peculiar to itself. It has had few owners and few major alterations, and is now the museum and headquarters of Historic Charleston Foundation. *Chamberlain photograph.*

For other illustrations, see color insert.

The elegant green room of the Russell House, like the formal rooms in many Charleston houses, is on the second floor and extends across the entire front of the house. Seven great windows stretch from floor to ceiling cornice. Their frames are beautifully ornamented, with unusual double, encased pilasters on either side. On a tea table made in Charleston c. 1800 is a French porcelain tea service strongly reflecting Russian influence. The Aubusson rug is also of c. 1800. The four armchairs are French and the pair of side chairs in front of the windows, Italian. Also from Italy is the table with scagliola top between the windows. Above it hangs an allegorical painting by Angelica Kauffmann (1740-1807).

History in towns: Beaufort, South Carolina

BY ROBERTA WRIGHT

BEAUFORT, ON PORT ROYAL ISLAND off the coast of South Carolina, is celebrating this spring the four-hundredth anniversary of the first attempt to colonize in the region. The Spaniards had led in exploring the deep-water channels and natural harbors of the barrier islands, but the first settlement there (it lasted only a few weeks, and was probably on Parris Island) was made by the Huguenot Jean Ribaut in 1562. He could find, he said, "No fayrer or fytter place."

Ruins or site markers of the forts built by the Huguenots, by the returning Spanish in 1564, and by Scotch Covenanters in 1684, survive as mute evidence of the early efforts at settlement of the offshore islands. It was the English who finally succeeded in establishing a lasting foothold, with Captain William Hilton's 1663 cruise into St. Helena Sound. A seaport town was ordered built, and about 1712 Beaufort (named in honor of Henry Somerset, Duke of Beaufort) was founded.

Colonists of this outer-island post had to be a hardy lot to endure the isolation and the frequent Indian raids. They built their town with protection the foremost consideration: at first Beaufort consisted of a blockhouse surrounded by a few dwellings. The simple frame house built by one Thomas Hepworth in 1717 is a reminder of this era. Its high basement walls are provided with slits through which the settlers could fire at attacking Indians. Another surviving example of early architecture is Retreat Plantation house, constructed about 1740 of a local building material called tabby—a mixture of oyster shells, lime, sand, and salt water.

Cultivation and exportation of indigo produced a plantation system in the Beaufort-Port Royal region, molding the new town and its buildings. Plantation owners in the surrounding area built town houses within Beaufort. Here, with their families, they retreated during the summer months to escape the humid heat of the malarial marshes.

Beaufort was a small but thriving port town at the onset of the Revolution. It was also almost defenseless, and it fell to an invading British fleet early in the war; according to a contemporary account, "All society came to an end with each family keeping close to its plantation." Recovery after the war, however, was remarkable. Fortunes were amassed by planters who gradually substituted rice and the famous Sea Island cotton for indigo; and as the city's wealth grew, its social and cultural level rose to new heights. During this prosperous era handsome houses were built on the waterfront or along the oak-shaded streets.

Designed in the popular Adam or Greek Revival styles, these houses combined functionalism with beauty. Foundation walls, often with arcaded openings, formed the ground level and served as protection against high water during storms. Stately columns supported wide verandas extending across the first and second stories. Tall windows let in the salt breezes and outside shutters cut off the midday sunlight. Huge, high-ceilinged rooms opened into broad halls for large parties and receptions. Typical of the residences built in this romantic period is the Edmund Rhett house, celebrated for its part in the South's secession from the Union. Another of the city's

Retreat Plantation's house was built c. 1740 by a latter-day Huguenot, Jean de la Gaye, on a branch of Battery Creek about six miles from Beaufort. Its twenty-two-inch walls are of tabby, the chimneys are brick, and the roof, slate. The porch is probably a somewhat later addition. Camellias and azaleas bloom in a formal brick-walled garden on the east side of the house. *Residence of Mr. and Mrs. Antonio Ponvert.*

The John Joyner Smith House, overlooking Beaufort Bay; c. 1813. The front door of this handsome Greek Revival house is an interesting feature. Designed simply to enhance the façade, it does not open. French windows give access from the veranda, and the principal entrance to the house is on the side. During the Civil War this house was used as headquarters by the occupying Union forces. *Residence of the Honorable Angus Fordham, mayor of Beaufort, and Mrs. Fordham.*

landmarks, the Johnson-Danner house, was complete except for marble mantels and ironwork at the beginning of the Civil War. One of the few Beaufort homes redeemed after the war by the original owners, it has remained in the same family. Its dignity of design and location make it a perfect show place.

Beaufort homes were built with the legendary Southern hospitality in mind. Here George Washington visited his friend Henry de Saussure, first director of the United States Mint. A reception was held in Beaufort for Lafayette, who spoke from the porch of the Verdier home on lower Bay Street.

During the Civil War the proud little city was occupied by Union soldiers for four long years, and it was virtually deserted by its residents. The men had left to fight on other fronts, and their families were evacuated by boat. Federal troops took over the public buildings and were billeted in the mansions. St. Helena's Church was used for a hospital, its flat tombstones turned into operating tables. The Baptist Church, a classic example of Greek Revival architecture, suffered the indig-

nity of having boards stretched from its balconies to form a second floor for the accommodation of wounded invaders. Occupation served a purpose, however: the town was spared destruction by Sherman's army.

Property owners who returned after the war found their homes being sold for taxes. According to legend, when the Fripp house was being auctioned a Frenchman living in town bought it, kissed the original owner on both cheeks, presented him with the deed, and disappeared without waiting to be thanked. But for most of the city reconstruction was slow and painful. Eventually the town achieved a measure of security, and by 1891 the Marine Corps had established its huge recruit training depot on Parris Island, where the French Huguenots had set up their first fort in 1562.

Time has wrought other changes. The chain of islands is linked by a system of bridges; modern roads have made accessible great expanses of beach front; convenient boat landings are available for boatmen. Yet the serene beauty of the locality is untouched. Leisure and graciousness are inherent in the Carolina low country.

Beaufort Arsenal, 1851. A fortlike structure surrounded by a crenelated brick wall and a row of palmettos, the present arsenal was constructed on the foundation of the 1780 original. Since 1851 it has been in continuous use. At present the sprawling building is headquarters for the local National Guard company; one wing houses the Beaufort Museum, where the relics on display date from 1711.

Thomas Hepworth House, 1717; built on one of the first grants of land in the city and believed to be its oldest house. The tabby foundation of the carefully restored white clapboard original portion (there are later additions) has, in the back, slits for muskets. *Residence of Mr. and Mrs. Somers Pringle.*

Fraser House, 1804; built by Frederick Fraser of the old Carolina family. Typical of low-country architecture, with its high basement, symmetrical chimneys, double balconies, and outside double stairway, this house in the middle of Beaufort is one of few survivors in a once aristocratic neighborhood. Of interest is the fine Palladian window on the upper veranda. *Residence of Dr. and Mrs. Maurice Matteson.*

Lafayette Building, 1795. When John Mark Verdier built this house on Bay Street, in the heart of Beaufort's business district, he extended its portico out into the street so he could see his ships at the dock. It has been brought back within bounds without harm to the building's basic lines. Lafayette was entertained at the Verdier home when he visited Beaufort in 1825. The building is now being restored.

Tidewater; late 1830's, with an 1892 addition. Said to have been cut in half and moved by barge before the Civil War from Lady's Island to its present site on Beaufort's "Point." The upper ceilings of this house are six inches higher than those on the lower floor, and the fanlight over the porch door on the second story is much more delicate than that below, which has given rise to the theory that the house was put back together upside down. Of wood on a high brick foundation, the house boasts a modillion cornice and six identical broad marble mantels. *Residence of Mr. and Mrs. W. Brantley Harvey.*

The Edmund Rhett House, better known as Secession House, is of modified Greek Revival architecture on a foundation of tabby; it has seen many changes since it was built as a two-story house of tabby in 1743. The walls of the second floor were replaced by clapboards and a third floor was added, all mounted on an arcaded basement with iron grills in the arches. The two-deck piazza has Corinthian columns above Ionic. An interesting feature of the interior is the elaborate matching cornice work in all the rooms. When the Ordinance of Secession was signed in 1860, Edmund Rhett occupied this historic residence; he was the brother of United States Senator Robert Barnwell Rhett, who has been called the father of Secession; the place was a hotbed of sentiment for Southern independence for many years. During the Civil War it was occupied by Federal soldiers. *Residence of Mr. and Mrs. Claude McLeod.*

Marshlands, 1814; built by Dr. James Robert Verdier, member of a family prominent in Beaufort since the eighteenth century. This striking example of late Adam design was made famous in Francis Griswold's best-selling novel *The Sea Island Lady*. Set like a jewel in a garden almost surrounded by water, the house has been carefully restored. *Residence of Mr. and Mrs. Sterling Harris.*

Means House, early 1850's; built on the Point by Colonel Edward Means. The large brick residence has exceptionally graceful semicircular entrance steps and portico. On one side is a double veranda supported by many columns and edged with delicate balustrades. *Residence of Mr. and Mrs. George Tucker.*

Intricate ceiling plasterwork in Greek Revival motifs is one of the beauties of the Baptist Church of Beaufort, built in 1844. The heavy acanthus-leaf design of the border, weakened by age, was meticulously restored with the rest of the sanctuary after hurricane damage in 1959. A double set of Doric columns supports the balconies, and the tall oval windows are louvered.

National stone: the Cumberland Road and American architecture

BY JAMES D. VAN TRUMP

A NOTEWORTHY DISPLAY of early American stone vernacular architecture is still to be found along the old Cumberland Road, or National Pike (now part of U. S. Route 40), which was constructed between 1811 and 1828 by the federal government to connect Cumberland, Maryland, with Wheeling, West Virginia. Carried eventually as far as Illinois, this road became a kind of American Appian Way, the chief land route between the eastern seaboard and the new western country. Following in part the old eighteenth-century wilderness roads Nemacolin's Path and Braddock's Road, it was first projected by Washington and advanced under the interested patronage of Jefferson, Gallatin, and Clay. Until the advent of the railroad age around 1850, it was clamorous with traffic, both passenger and freight; Presidents, statesmen, and pioneers, drovers, and traveling salesmen passed over it in an endless cavalcade. Today, after a long period of decline in the later nineteenth century, it now carries trailer trucks and tourists past the old Pike scenery of inns and houses, churches and bridges, all massively constructed in stone.

The Allegheny Mountains in this region are underlaid by beds of limestone, sandstone, and quartzite, which provided an abundance of building material for local stonemasons long before the road was planned. At first the highway was itself of stone, composed of a lower course of great boulders covered by a layer of smaller stones; later it was macadamized and today it is a concrete arrow winging across the ridges in super-highway fashion, while great loops of the old road, now disused, wander off into the countryside. The modern traveler should not neglect these abandoned stretches, for it is there, very often, that local stone architecture is to be seen at its best.

The mountains place their signature on the road at its very beginning, in the Narrows just outside of Cumberland, where great folds of exposed rock strata —like prehistoric baroque scrolls—swoop down upon the winding ribbon of concrete. Gradually the road climbs into the ridges: Big and Little Savage Mountains, Negro Mountain, Keyser's Ridge. Here begins also the procession of stone inns which were once so prominent a feature of the Pike.

Among these mountains and valleys, bridges were absolutely necessary, and today their deserted stone arches web the abandoned stretches of the old road. West of Washington, Pennsylvania, is still to be found one of the famous "S" bridges (this one constructed in 1818) whose skewed span snakes the road over a small creek. Engineers of the day found it cheaper to build these bridges at an angle to the flow of the stream. The largest of the Pike structures still extant is the single-span Little Crossings bridge (Fig. 1) erected in 1813 over the Casselman, or Castleman, River in Maryland.

Fig. 1. Little Crossings bridge (1813) over the Castleman River in Maryland, largest of the bridges remaining along the old Cumberland Road. *All photographs by James H. Cook.*

It is a graceful structure, whose almost Chinese amplitude of arch gives it a curiously exotic aspect against its hillside background.

Many of the stone inns, dating from the early decades of the nineteenth century, have been converted to other uses, but they are still recognizable. All western Pennsylvania architecture has a massive, rugged character of its own, but the Pike taverns have an almost military strength which is strangely impressive. Modeled usually after the center-hall, five-bay, two-story-and-attic Georgian house of the previous century, the type seems to be reduced here to the simplest terms, an elemental statement of thick-walled shelter. Without adornment save for an occasional fanlight, these structures depend for their effect on sheer bulk. The Krepps Inn (1822-1830) (Fig. 2) at Malden near Brownsville has lost its front veranda, and can be seen in all its original starkness. The great twin chimneys connected by roof curtains at the gable ends, the enormously thick walls, and the projecting wings at the back are features common to the type.

Small grace notes along the National Road are the tollhouses. At Addison in Pennsylvania, just across the Maryland border, is one of the three remaining structures of this type which were erected when the state took over the Pike in 1835 (Fig. 3). Hexagonal, it is the only one constructed of stone; with its wide windows and veranda it has almost the look of an eighteenth-century teahouse or garden pavilion perched beside a brackish stream of concrete. This charming little building is well preserved by the Great Crossings chapter of the Daughters of the American Revolution.

One of the most fascinating towns in the region is Brownsville, formerly Redstone, where the Pennsylvania section of the highway hurtles abruptly through depths of historical strata, past a plane of modern manufacturing, to the valley of the Monongahela River. Here somnolent and decaying streets recall only faintly the early nineteenth-century importance of the place which once rivaled, briefly, Pittsburgh.

Among the forlorn towers looking out from its hills, the spire of St. Peter's Roman Catholic Church (1845) (Fig. 4) crowns a structure whose primitive neo-fourteenth-century mass seems to have penetrated Pugin's revivalism to the very roots of the style. Its architect is unknown, and its stripped, abstracted forms are very similar in spirit to those of the roadside inns. Unlike them, however, the

Fig. 5.   Doorway of Brashear Tavern (1796), Brownsville.

Fig. 6.   Bowman's Castle (c. 1800-1850), Brownsville.

Fig. 7.   LeMoyne House (1812), Washington, Pennsylvania, headquarters of the Washington County Historical Society.

church is a structural reminiscence brought directly from Europe.

That there was often little difference in form between the inn and the private house may be seen in the Market Street hostelry built by Basil Brashear in 1796. With its stone façade flush with the street, it is a provincial version of the three-bay Georgian town house with hall and entrance at one side. The classical fanlighted doorway (Fig. 5) displays pilasters whose charmingly wayward details foreshadow the vagaries of the Victorian turning lathe.

Looming over the site of Fort Burd, about which the town grew in the late eighteenth century, is the rambling gabled and towered mass of Bowman's Castle (Fig. 6), or Nemacolin Towers, a western Pennsylvania version of the Hudson River country house. Built mostly of brick around a small stone core between c. 1800 and the 1850's, this highly romantic blending of Gothic and Tuscan villa architecture was once the house of the town's leading citizens. Measures are under consideration by both the state and the community to preserve it as a local monument, but it remains to be seen whether they will be successful.

At Washington, Pennsylvania, on Maiden Street, which is part of Route 40, is a handsome early Federal building, the LeMoyne House (Fig. 7), now the headquarters of the Washington County Historical Society. Built in 1812 by a prominent local citizen, Dr. John Julius Le-Moyne, it has an asymmetrical façade flush with the street, a small portico with Ionic pillars, and a row of low attic lights at the cornice, where there was at one time an open gallery. The interior woodwork in the principal rooms, while sophisticated in concept, retains a certain provincial quality in the execution; there is here an echo of the late Georgian style of the eastern part of the state, but the exterior treatment foreshadows the Greek Revival. The house is fairly well preserved and may be visited.

After Washington, the road descends to Wheeling and the Ohio River, attended by the usual inns and an occasional bridge. In the Ohio flatlands on the other side of the river there is little stone architecture visible along the highway and certainly nothing of the mountain type. The original Cumberland Road, which began in elemental stone at the Narrows, ends appropriately with the great masonry arches of the Ellet-Roebling suspension bridge (1846-1854) at Wheeling.

Domestic architecture in Middle Tennessee

BY ALBERT W. HUTCHISON JR., *Chairman, Historic Sites Federation of Tennessee*

THE FIRST SETTLERS to come to Middle Tennessee arrived in December of 1779 at the place on the Cumberland River that is now called Nashville (see p. 380). There they found rich valleys and rolling hills abounding in timber, limestone, brick clay, and other builder's resources. They also encountered several unfavorable factors, chiefly immense distances to civilized centers, lack of transportation facilities, and—more serious—ceaseless and murderous Indian warfare which endured until the turn of the century.

On this frontier the log cabin was the only type of building for several years. Log structures were used for homes, forts, courthouses, and jails. Four or five men could build a small cabin in a few days with materials found at the site and with the implements every settler had—an ax, hatchet, and a knife. Logs from seventy or eighty small trees, alternately stacked, notched, and chinked, would build a one-room cabin sixteen by twenty feet. The addition of a second cabin, ten feet or so away under a common roof, formed the popular double-cabin-with-dogtrot, so admirably suited to the climate, the materials, and the labor supply. The two-story version, with the dogtrot (or breezeway) enclosed and converted into a central hall with a stairway, and with an outside chimney at each end, rapidly became the prototype of the later farmhouses of the region as well as of the grander houses.

For the next hundred years, the architecture of Middle Tennessee falls into three broad periods, interrupted by the ten years of the Civil War and Reconstruction: the transitional structures of pioneer days from 1779 to 1820; the classical revivals between 1820 and 1860; and the

eclectic architecture of the Victorian era from 1870 to 1890. Hence there exists today an impressive array of houses, beginning with dwellings of the early 1780's. Some are strikingly handsome, some are well preserved, while others are surprisingly run-down, but taken together they present a remarkably complete picture of the architecture and way of life of a region that is now approaching the two-hundredth anniversary of its settlement.

In 1784, near Hendersonville, General Daniel Smith built Rock Castle (Fig. 1), the first of several stone houses in the area and the first house of importance erected in this part of the country. Cragfont (Pl. VIII) near Gallatin, built by General James Winchester between 1798 and 1802, exemplifies the peak of pioneer grandeur in the use of stone. Both houses show the marks of skilled workmen and have roots in the stone houses of Pennsylvania and the Georgian houses of Virginia.

The first brick house in the area, built by Captain William Bowen in 1787, stands vacant and deteriorating near Goodlettsville. Severe in design, it has novel features in its twin entrance doors and lack of a central hall. This house marks the beginning of the use of brick, hand-molded and kilned on the site, as a building material. François André Michaux, a French botanist, noted that in 1802 Nashville had only seven or eight brick houses and about one hundred and twenty constructed of wood, but the use of brick increased rapidly until it became the dominant building material of the region.

By 1800 the streets of Nashville began to take the form of a town plan that was to become typical in Middle Tennessee: a square enclosing a courthouse or a monument

Fig. 1. Rock Castle, a limestone mansion near Hendersonville, is one of the earliest houses of importance to be built in Tennessee. The foundations were laid in 1784 by General Daniel Smith (see p. 378); the rear ell was not built until 1793. The entrance portico, added in the 1850's, obscures the dissymmetry of the windows on either side of the entry. The 1887 slate roof replaced an earlier one of wood shingle. Rock Castle and eighteen acres of the original five-thousand-acre estate were purchased by the State of Tennessee in 1969 as a historic site to be managed and restored by the Friends of Rock Castle. *Photograph by the Historic American Buildings Survey.*

Fig. 2. Oaklands was built between the early 1800's and c. 1855. A succession of styles is reflected here: from farmhouse (the original two-room house of c. 1800 is not visible here) to Italianate villa, with a Romanesque revival veranda and entrance portico. It stands on part of a 1786 North Carolina grant, purchased in 1798 by Lieutenant Colonel Hardy Murfree, for whom the city of Murfreesboro was named. This house remained in the possession of Dr. James Maney, Murfree's son-in-law, and his family until 1884. The city of Murfreesboro purchased twenty-nine remaining acres of the original estate in 1957 for use as a municipal park and two years later deeded the mansion and garden to the Oaklands Association to be restored and maintained as a historic site. *Except as noted, photographs are by Helga Photo Studio.*

Fig. 3. The Sam Davis Home at Symrna near Nashville, in which the Confederate hero lived during his boyhood, is an excellent example of a Middle Tennessee plantation. Behind the pedimented portico and balcony stands the original 1810 log structure with its outside end chimneys. The poplar siding, rear wing, and L-shape rear porch were added in 1847. In 1927 the state bought the property and since 1930 it has been managed by the Sam Davis Memorial Association as trustees for the State of Tennessee.

was the central public amenity for a rectangular grid of commercial structures and town houses. Radiating trails, later turnpikes, to distant communities led past rural plantations which from 1820 on would become numerous and substantial. The town house began as, and remained, a detached, single-family structure rather than a row house, and like the rural house was a simplified version of the Georgian (Fig. 1) or, less frequently, the Federal style. The trend to the detached dwelling may have stemmed from the fear of fire, the desire for space and freedom, the need for cross ventilation, and the fact that land could be purchased at a low price.

The stately Greek revival, popularized in America by such architects as Benjamin Henry Latrobe, gained wide acceptance in the 1820's and 1830's, and reached a high point of white-pillared grandeur in Tennessee shortly after William Strickland, a pupil of Latrobe, moved from Philadelphia to Tennessee in 1845 to build the classical Tennessee state capitol (see cover and p. 377). With in-

creased travel to the Continent, the last decade of the antebellum period saw wide acceptance of the magnificent Italian villa, often with an Italianate tower derived from the medieval campanile. This revival may also reflect the influence of Strickland, who not only was well versed in the classical tradition but also had traveled in Italy. The early Gothic revival was confined almost entirely to ecclesiastical and institutional buildings.

A variation of the earlier double-cabin-with-dogtrot gained considerable favor in Tennessee during this period, and can be found in several styles including the neoclassical and Gothic revival. This version of the local prototype was characterized by a recessed entry, cast-iron balcony, pedimented portico with two-story columns, and pilasters at the corners and at the entry. An example of this neoclassical adaptation may be seen in elaborate form in Rattle and Snap (Pl. IX) and Belmont (Fig. 6). A Gothicized variation is the Athenaeum (Fig. 5).

The Civil War stopped construction and ended an

Pl. VIII. Cragfont, begun in 1798 and completed four years later, was the home of General James Winchester. The handsome mantel and cabinetry of the parlor have been attributed to Frank Weatherred, a carpenter known to have done much of the woodwork at Cragfont. The stenciling on the walls was reproduced from a faded remnant of the original design done by an itinerant artist. The house was purchased by the state in 1958 and is maintained by the Sumner County chapter of the APTA.

Pl. IX. (Facing page.) Rattle and Snap, near Columbia, is the last built and most ornate of the Polk houses. The designer of this house is unknown, but it was completed in 1845 for George Polk, a relative of President James K. Polk. The name Rattle and Snap was applied to the estate after it reputedly changed hands several times in one night in the mid-1800's during a gambling game; its name was changed to Oakland Hall in the late nineteenth century. Mr. and Mrs. Oliver M. Babcock, the present owners, purchased the estate in 1953 and have restored not only its former grandeur but also its colorful earlier name.

Fig. 6. Belmont, in Nashville, designed in the style of an Italian Renaissance villa with Greek revival details, was built in 1850 for the wealthy widow of Major Isaac Franklin. She had recently remarried and was Mrs. J. A. S. Acklen when the house was built. The walls of the house are of brick, stuccoed and scored in an ashlar pattern. The house was purchased in 1890 from the estate of Mrs. Acklen by Belmont College. The mansion and grounds still contain some of the gazebos, hitching posts, statuary, and paths and the picturesque water tower that were part of the original estate. *HABS photograph.*

Fig. 7. Belle Meade, a regal Greek revival plantation house six miles west of Nashville, was built for General William Giles Harding in 1853 on the foundation of an earlier structure also called Belle Meade and destroyed by fire. The house is constructed of brick covered with stucco scored in an ashlar pattern. The square columns and portico, surmounted by a delicate pediment and acroteria, are made of limestone quarried on the site. Owned by the State of Tennessee since 1953, the mansion and its twenty-four remaining acres are managed by the Association for the Preservation of Tennessee Antiquities.

Fig. 8. Two Rivers, built by David McGavock in 1859, takes its name from its fertile site which lies at the junction of the Stones River with the Cumberland a few miles west of Nashville. McGavock was his own architect and builder. This house represents an outstanding example of the early Italianate style in Middle Tennessee. The house is now maintained by the city of Nashville and the land is under development for a park and high school. *HABS photograph.*

Nathan Vaught, whose unpublished diary in the state archives sheds much light on structures in Maury County, listed himself as a carpenter in the 1850 census. With the mason Levi Ketchum laying the brick, he built perhaps fifty houses before the Civil War. Briscoe Vannoy, a Gallatin architect in the 1840's, unsuccessfully submitted plans for the First Presbyterian Church in Nashville in competition with William Strickland (see ANTIQUES, August 1971, p. 222). He is listed in the 1850 census together with L. W. Sampson, an architect born in New Hampshire in 1804, as living in Clarksville. Other architects listed in the 1850 census include F. Stratton (b. 1810 in Virginia) of Spring Hill, who may have assisted in planning the elegant Cheairs houses; James A. Gadsy (b. 1800 in Virginia) of Franklin; and from Nashville, Adolphus Heiman (b. 1809 in Prussia), William Strickland, and his son, Francis W. Strickland, a draftsman. Other architects not listed in the census but working in Nashville in 1850 were H. M. Ackeroid and H. M. Brown & Sons.

Certainly the two most famous architects of the period were William Strickland and Adolphus Heiman (see ANTIQUES, August 1971, p. 223, Figs. 2, 4). Gideon Shryock, famous Kentucky architect and former pupil of Strickland, may have done work in Tennessee. He and Heiman entered the competition for the Tennessee state capitol, which was awarded to Strickland.

In the 1870's C. G. Rosenplanter of Memphis, formerly of Louisville, Kentucky, was working in Clarksville, primarily designing several handsome churches. By 1880 the city directory list of Nashville architects included T. Brennan, J. H. Cochrane, W. H. Cusack, W. K. Dobson, W. F. Foster, John Lewis, J. L. Smith, W. C. Smith, H. C. Thompson, and P. J. Williamson.

The number of architects continued to increase, and by October 1896 Middle Tennessee was sufficiently attractive for Nashville to play host to the thirtieth annual convention of the American Institute of Architects. Architects from all over the country, including many who had designed buildings for the Chicago World's Fair of 1893, met at the Maxwell House, visited the Hermitage, and praised William Strickland and his capitol.

The Arkansas Territorial Capitol, Little Rock

IN THE HEART of the city of Little Rock, Arkansas, is a block of small frame and brick buildings, set among lawns and gardens behind a white picket fence, which forms a striking contrast to the big cotton warehouses that surround it. This is the Arkansas Territorial Capitol Restoration, consisting of some of the first houses built in the region. The Capitol, built in 1820, was the meeting place of the last Territorial Legislature in 1835, and scene of the drafting of the state constitution. The three dwelling houses with their dependencies were built before 1830. Though constructed when the Greek Revival was coming into fashion, they reflect rather the southern eighteenth-century tradition, translated in simplified terms to the frontier.

The Restoration was created and is owned by the state. Begun in 1939, the project was completed in 1941, when the buildings were opened to the public. In restoring them it was necessary to remove certain architectural additions and many coats of paint,

NOLAND HOUSE. Rear view, showing part of the garden, the well, the original owner's office at left, the kitchen at right, and a corner of the Capitol at far right. This low brick house with its columned porch and detached dependencies is in the southern tradition.

Photographs by Earl Saunders

BEDROOM, Noland House. The original owner of this house was Lieutenant C. F. M. Noland, who was delegated to carry the first State Constitution of Arkansas to Washington. He probably brought such furniture as this from the east, or up-river from New Orleans.

TAVERN ROOM, Capitol. All ceiling beams, upstairs and down, are beaded. Here the walls are sheathed, and a simple mantel finishes the fireplace. Furniture includes, suitably, windsor chairs and benches — that at right amusingly crude. The cupboard or "safe" has tin panels pierced in a bold eagle-and-star design. Note the turkey wing for sweeping the hearth.

THE CAPITOL. Built in 1820 of oak logs covered with cypress siding. In 1834 it was remodeled and refinements of architectural detail were added.

but the buildings themselves were in excellent condition. They are now preserved in their original materials and original appearance, outfitted with appropriate furnishings. Many of the latter, obtained from descendants of the first owners, had been used in their present setting over a century ago. In the words of Newton B. Drury, director of the National Park Service, the Arkansas Capitol Restoration is commendable for its "historical perception, fidelity, and restraint."

— A. W.

COUNCIL ROOM, Capitol. Here the walls have been stripped of sheathing and plaster to show log construction. The furnishings are the kind of thing made and used on the frontier in the days of settlement, 1820's—1840's, and now generally called American Empire.

CONWAY HOUSE. One-story frame-building, the first residence of Elias N. Conway, fifth governor of the state. The two-part paneled door is framed with recessed lights.

PARLOR, Conway House. The woodwork is the simple, provincial expression of the classic taste of the time. The sofa, clock, and table are equally appropriate to their setting.

THE STABLE. Adjacent to the Noland House is the small, steep-roofed stable which now houses old vehicles.

Log houses in Wisconsin

BY RICHARD W. E. PERRIN, *F.A.I.A.*

Historic buildings preservation officer, American Institute of Architects

LOG CONSTRUCTION of houses was introduced into the Delaware Valley by the Swedes as early as 1638, but this form of architectural construction did not spread much beyond that geographic region until the early eighteenth century. The long-popular belief that early English settlers chose as their type of dwelling the log cabin that was later so conspicuous a feature of the North American frontier was demolished by Harold R. Shurtleff in his pioneering study *The Log Cabin Myth* (1939). Rather, they built in the traditional English styles they had known at home: framed wooden buildings, roofed with thatch or cedar shingle, and filled between outer wall and interior sheathing with nogging. Solid timber wall construction was never indigenous to the British Isles, and was not used by seventeenth-century English colonists except in garrisons and blockhouses near the end of the century.

The house of horizontal logs laid in a rectangle, notched together at the corners, and chinked with clay, was brought into the Colonies by the first settlers from northern Europe. With the eventual failure of the Swedish settlement on the Delaware, log construction of houses did not spread through the Colonies during the remainder of the seventeenth century. According to Shurtleff, the Scotch-Irish who began arriving here in large numbers after 1718 seem to have been the first English-speaking group to adopt it. The Germans, independently of the Swedes, made a fresh introduction of the log house in the Colonies about 1710. From the Germans and Scotch-Irish, such construction spread rapidly and by the time of the Revolution reached as far west as the mountains of Tennessee. Obviously suited to the densely forested new country, where trees had to be felled for tillage, the log house gradually became the typical house of the later frontiersman.

The earliest examples, usually one story high with loft, had gable roofs covered with shakes or bark. Such a house would contain one room which served as kitchen, sitting room, and dining room, with sleeping quarters in one corner sometimes partitioned off by nothing more than a blanket. The loft, approached by a ladder in one corner

Fig. 1. Joseph Goodrich house, Yankee-type log house; built c. 1835, Milton, Rock County. *Photographs by the author.*

Fig. 2. John Petty cabin, Yankee-type log house; built c. 1835, near Aztalan, Jefferson County.

Fig. 3. Christian Turck house, German-type log house;
built in 1835 in Germantown,
located southeast of Kirchhayn, Washington County.

Fig. 4. Fourteen-sided log barn, German type;
built c. 1895 by Henry Rademacher, on Musser Flowage
of the Big Elk River, east of Phillips, Price County.

of the cabin, was commonly used as sleeping space for the children. In larger cabins a wood partition sometimes divided the space into rooms; and, as time went on, lean-to kitchens might be added, giving a salt-box profile.

Seventeenth- and eighteenth-century log-house survivals in their original condition have nearly vanished and can, therefore, be best seen in restorations and reconstructions. Among the finest of these is Schoenbrunn in eastern Ohio, where the mid-eighteenth-century log houses of a Moravian colony have been faithfully reproduced on the original foundations. Under the tutelage of German Moravian missionaries these cabins were built by Indian converts. Structurally they reflect the German preference for fairly wide spaces between logs chinked with clay and pargeted with lime plaster. The Scotch-Irish adaptation of the Swedish technique of tight-fitting, squared logs may be seen in the early nineteenth-century cabins at Spring Mill State Park near Mitchell, Indiana. Here substantial restoration is evident, but the cabins are the original fabric, not reproductions.

Moving farther into the Middle West, original nineteenth-century log houses in various states of repair can best be seen in that part of the old Northwest Territory which is now Wisconsin. Interestingly, among the first permanent settlers in this area were New England Yankees, who brought with them a method of log construction that had been learned from German and Swedish immigrants and then modified in various ways. In addition to the Yankee log cabin, Wisconsin exhibits three basic types which may be classified as German, Slavic, and Scandinavian. Log construction ended in southern Wisconsin by 1870 but continued in the northern and more remote forest areas of the state well into the early twentieth century.

Two of the most interesting Yankee log-cabin survivals are the Joseph Goodrich house at Milton in Rock County (Fig. 1) and the John Petty cabin at Aztalan in Jefferson County (Fig. 2). Each is a small one-room structure with a large open-hearth fireplace at one end. Both were built about the time Wisconsin was established as a separate territory in 1836.

One of the best specimens of early German log architecture is the completely unspoiled Christian Turck house near Kirchhayn in Washington County (Fig. 3). Built in 1835 of cedar logs felled in the adjoining swamp, it has a salt-box profile. The house is set into the slope of the land so that its back, with the broad roof expanse, is turned to the north and the front is opened up to the south. It has a central-hall plan with a room on either side. Some of the floor timbers are ash and oak, and a longitudinal summer beam runs through the middle of the house at each floor level. The spaces between the summer beams and the floor beams resting upon them are filled with clay and rye straw. Wide spaces between the wall logs are also heavily chinked with clay and rye straw, covered with lime plaster—done deliberately to permit recalking as necessary because of shrinking of the wood.

Barns and other farm buildings were also built in the German style of log construction. One of the most unusual is a fourteen-sided dairy barn built about 1895 (Fig. 4).

Slavic log structures in Wisconsin, chiefly the work of Bohemian and Polish settlers, resemble the German in a number of important respects. Not many of these log buildings remain as originally built, although a number of farmhouses still in use are actually old log houses covered with modern sheathing. Surviving log barns are less apt to have been so modified; an excellent example is the well-preserved Hashek barn near Myra in Washington County (Figs. 5, 6). Of squared and carefully fitted cedar logs, it was built by an early Bohemian settler around 1855. The logs were laid with spaces between but never chinked, presumably to permit good ventilation for the hay.

The most significant Scandinavian log architecture in Wisconsin is that introduced by Norwegian and Finnish settlers. In Norway Township, Racine County, stands one of the last remnants of the old Muskego settlement, the John Bergen log house (Fig. 7). Built about 1843 by Osten Gullickson Meland, one of the first arrivals there, it is situated on a gentle rise of land overlooking an old tamarack swamp. The longitudinal axis of the house is northeast-southwest, and a four-foot wide *sval*, or gallery, extends along the entire northwest side. The walls are laid up of carefully hewn timbers five inches thick and averaging eleven inches in height, slightly rounded on the inside and chamfered on the outside. While pine and spruce were almost universally used in the Norwegian homeland, the Bergen house was built of white oak logs. The ceiling of the first floor is only six feet high and has exposed six-by-six-inch hewn beams placed thirty-two inches apart. In the *stue*, or parlor, the beams were stained with natural black-walnut juice, then waxed and polished.

In northwestern Wisconsin, the Getto house in Oulu Township, Bayfield County, is an excellent example of traditional and primitive architecture carried into the twentieth century (Figs. 8, 9). It is a typical Finnish dwelling built of squared black-ash logs and follows the ancient Nordic hearth-house pattern of three adjoining rooms of equal size. After the wall logs and roof had been placed, the whole building was left unfinished for about a year so that the walls could settle, each log in the wall fitting still more tightly upon the one below. Then the door and window openings were cut and grooved in such a way that the logs could continue to sink without affecting the openings. A strip of woolen cloth was laid between the logs as a sort of gasket, but no chinking or daubing of any kind was employed.

The area of Douglas and Bayfield Counties is one of the few places in the country where Finnish log saunas are still seen (Figs. 10, 11), though in rapidly decreasing numbers. Small

Fig. 5. Hashek log barn, Bohemian type; built c. 1855, near Myra, Washington County.

Fig. 6. Detail of Hashek barn, showing dovetail joining of cedar logs.

rooms were often added and the sauna thereby became far more than a steam bath. Because of its warmth it was used for germinating barley and drying meat, flax, herbs, and berries, and it served as a workshop where candles were made. Spruce and willow bark was hung here; when dry and brittle it was splintered and put into the tanning brine to cure hides.

Wisconsin is the site of another kind of log construction rarely found elsewhere, which is graphically called "stovewood." Though the technique was introduced as early as 1848 by New England settlers, the best examples of stovewood construction date from the latter part of the century. Structurally, this system of building involved the laying up of short lengths of whole or split logs in a bed of lime mortar, giving the appearance of a well-stacked woodpile. Usually less than two feet in depth, these walls were extremely durable and made for a comfortable interior for both houses and barns. The best specimens are to be found in Door, Oconto, and Forest Counties in northern Wisconsin (Fig. 12). The ethnic origins of the builders suggest a German provenance for this type of construction, but positive identification of its source must await further exploration.

As the frontier moved westward, the log house became a universal architectural type. In Wisconsin it was introduced and then revised periodically by New England Yankees, Germans, Bohemians, Poles, Norwegians, and Finns to meet changing needs and conditions.

Fig. 7. John Bergen log house, Norwegian *tommerhus*; built in 1843 by Osten Gullickson Meland, in town of Norway, Racine County.

Fig. 8. Getto house, Finnish type; built c. 1900, in town of Oulu, Bayfield County.

Fig. 9. Detail of Getto house, showing dovetail joining of black swamp-ash logs.

Fig. 10. Soyring log sauna building,
Finnish type; built c. 1900,
near Maple, Douglas County.

Fig. 11. Detail of Soyring sauna,
showing joining of white swamp-cedar logs
in the round.

Fig. 12 Detail of Wendell Ison barn
with stovewood construction of
the walls; built c. 1895, near
Crandon, Forest County. Timber balks
used as quoins; walls originally
plastered inside and outside.

BY HELEN COMSTOCK

California adobes

IN THE YEAR 1845 a confidential message from the Secretary of State in Washington was read with great interest in a Monterey adobe, promising that should California assert her independence from Mexico, the United States would welcome a sister republic. That California, on the conclusion of the War with Mexico in 1846, was ready to welcome statehood rather than become a "sister republic" was due to the influence of American-born *Californios,* many of whom were New Englanders.

As in politics and business, New England influence made itself felt in architecture, with the result that Mexican-Colonial domestic architecture shows a dual character. There is, first, the Spanish-derived style, represented by the Casa Amesti in Monterey (below), as well as the de la Guerra house, now imbedded in the business section of Santa Barbara, the Aguirre house in San Diego, and the Rancho Olivos in Ventura, all illustrated by Hugh Morrison in his *Early American Architecture.* Secondly, there is the type which incorporated New England forms but employed basic adobe construction, as in the square-shaped Larkin House, Monterey (page 378). Occasionally the New England "salt box" is seen, with the long roof line extending to the rear, represented by the Whaling Station at Monterey.

Photograph by Moulin Studios

Adobe is a mixture of clay, sand, and water, with straw as a binder, poured into boxes or *adoberos* and dried in the sun. The result is a heavy slab of building material weighing fifty or more pounds and measuring about eighteen by ten by five inches. When laid in walls two to three feet thick it gives protection against heat or cold. Adobe brick was joined with mud mortar, or with lime mortar, covered with stucco and whitewashed. The usual form of the house was a long rectangle, or three rectangular wings around a patio. An inner veranda or *corredor* led from the patio to the house, and sometimes was used on the outer side as well. In the southern part of Mexican California, houses were usually one story high, but farther north, as at Monterey, San Juan, and Sonoma, many had two stories. Stairways were outside. Windows were unframed and unglazed and there was an iron grille outside, for protection, and a single heavy wooden shutter within, for warmth. Sometimes the grille was omitted in favor of a pair of heavy wooden outside shutters.

The New Englanders preferred sash windows with small panes of glass, sometimes twenty-light, as in the Larkin house where some of the original glass remains, or twenty-four-light, as at the Whaling Station. The in-terior stairway is thought to be a New England contribution to the California house, while fireplaces framed in simplified Adam mantels were certainly so. The Casa Alvarado (page 379) was built entirely in the Mexican style originally, and had no fireplaces, but two were added by Rev. Walter Colton, who was also the builder of Colton Hall at Monterey, where the Constitutional Convention met in 1849. Colton had arrived on one of Sloat's warships and remained to become the first American *alcalde* of Monterey.

Thomas O. Larkin, American consul at Monterey and agent of President Polk, was one of the most influential of the American-born *Californios*. In building his house at Monterey he departed from the usual rectangular form and employed instead the square lines of the late Georgian buildings he remembered in his native Massachusetts. As soon as mill-sawed lumber was available (it came from Australia via England), many house owners added wood siding to existing adobe walls to strengthen them, and in 1849 the first all-clapboard "adobe" was built in Monterey by Philip Roach.

New England influence is strong in the Trussell-Winchester adobe in Santa Barbara (page 380) which was built by Captain Horatio Gates Trussell of Orland, Maine,

Casa Amesti, Monterey. Built in 1825 by Don José Amesti, a Spanish Basque who came to Monterey at the age of thirty and married Prudenciana Vallejo, sister of General Vallejo. It was given in 1846 to their daughter, Carmen, and her husband, Don Santiago McKinley. The Casa Amesti is one of the finest examples of the *casa da puebla,* or town house, and shows the traditional rectangular form with veranda and balcony; the pair of narrow entrance doors is characteristic. Original furnishings are rare in the old adobes but their place is taken harmoniously by antiques from other regions. The French provincial furniture and eighteenth-century printed cottons are well suited to the simple background of a Mexican-Colonial interior, as seen in this bedroom at the Casa Amesti. *Mrs. Frances A. Elkins.*

Photograph by J. P. Graham

Photographs by Moulin Studios

Larkin House, Monterey. Bougainvillea, iris, and roses dominate the patio. Unlike most adobes, which were built around the patio, this square house has the patio at the side, enclosed in its own walls. Built in 1835 by Thomas O. Larkin, the house served as the American consulate from 1844 to 1846. None of the original furniture which Larkin brought from New England is now in the house, but the present owner, Larkin's grand-daughter, has inherited New England antiques from her Portsmouth, New Hampshire, ancestors. The portrait over the mantel is of Mrs. Larkin (Rachel Hobson Holmes) painted in Monterey by an unknown artist. *Mrs. H. W. Toulmin.*

Casa Alvarado, Monterey. Built shortly after the revolution of 1821, this house was the residence of Juan Bautista Alvarado, governor of California, 1836-1842. It was restored in 1946 for the present owners and is furnished chiefly with eighteenth-century Hepplewhite pieces. The exposed ceiling joists supporting planking represent a characteristic construction carried over into modern California architecture. The great depth of the adobe walls, which are covered with whitewashed plaster, may be noted at the window and door. The New England-style fireplace was added about 1848. *Dr. and Mrs. W. R. Heard.*

Casa Soberanes, Monterey. This house is generally called the "House with the Blue Gate" from the color of the entrance through the dense cypress hedge which entirely screens the house from the street. It was built in 1842 by Don José Estrada, ranking officer of the Presidio, and later sold to Don Mariano Soberanes. As his wife was a Vallejo, the house was frequently visited by the members of this famous family from the northern frontier. The Casa Soberanes has been lived in continuously to the present time and has some of its original Victorian furniture. The enclosed end of the veranda is typical, while a cantilevered balcony, without columns that extend all the way to the roof, is unusual. *Mrs. W. M. O'Donnell.*

Photograph by Karl Obert

Trussell-Winchester Adobe, Santa Barbara. Built in 1854 by a sea captain from Maine, this house combines Mexican and New England features, the center part being of adobe construction, the ends of wood frame and siding, while the shingle roof was one of the earliest in Santa Barbara. This house, the family home of Mrs. John Russel Hastings, has for the past ten years been dedicated by her to the work of the Santa Barbara Historical Society. *Mrs. John Russel Hastings.*

in 1854, and has been lived in by the Winchester family for over seventy years. Captain Trussell, a clipper ship master, came to California on the first steamship to enter Santa Barbara harbor. He married Ramona Burke and proceeded to build his own house, using some of the timbers of the shipwrecked *Winfield Scott,* lost off Anacapa Island while carrying homeward-bound gold seekers and their gold. He used the traditional adobe for the center of the house but wood-frame construction at the ends. Brass thresholds from the *Winfield Scott* are used under some of the interior doors. Among interesting items in the house are marine paintings by Captain Frank Thompson, a nephew of the Captain Thompson of the brig *Pilgrim,* in which Dana made the first part of his voyage described in *Two Years Before the Mast.*

The Trussell-Winchester adobe is the home of Mrs. John Russel Hastings, whose name is well known to readers of Antiques. In 1943 the Santa Barbara Historical Society was established here, through her generosity. To it she has brought her own collection of furniture and ceramics, and through her work the Society is bringing together a significant collection of Americana.

These carefully preserved adobes of the Mexican California period represent an interesting chapter in the development of regional styles of architecture. In them we find the traditional Spanish colonial style and adobe construction successfully blended with New England forms. The result is a unique and charming domestic architecture.

Photograph by Eby Photo Service

A camphorwood chest made in the Orient was one of the essentials of Mexican-Colonial household furnishings. Sometimes these chests came in graduated sizes. The leather which covered them came originally from California, and they were decorated with designs adapted to the taste of the western market. This chest was owned by Clementine Zimmerman Langenberger who was born in New Orleans in 1842 and came to California in 1848. *Charles W. Bowers Memorial Museum, Santa Ana.*